Praise

'Such an excellent book †
read "just one more chaṛ
The BELONG model helps create the stɾuᴄɪᴜɪᴇ
form necessary to facilitate the delivery of the DE&I
agenda within any organisation, and the aides-
memoires at the end of each chapter to instigate
action are very useful.'

> — **Robert Mason**, Head of Technology
> Programme Deliver, Guide Dogs for the
> Blind

'*The Inclusion Edge* can and will help you to make
your organisation a great place for everyone who
works there. The BELONG model is a step-by-
step process to help you make a whole series of
discoveries in creating a truly inclusive workplace.'

> — **Kathryn Jacob**, CEO, Pearl & Dean

'From page one Mary demonstrates how her own
personal experiences have made her uniquely
qualified to write this book. The blend of personal
and professional knowledge delivered in a digestible
manner holds your attention throughout. Any leader
wanting to do more for DE&I in their organisation
and unsure where to start or how to maintain
momentum should read this book.'

> — **Steven Cochrane**, Director of Data and
> Analytics, Flutter Entertainment

'Mary writes with authority and authenticity. *The Inclusion Edge* is a helpful, easy-to-understand guide for managers seeking to develop understanding of inclusion in the twenty-first century workplace.'
— **Jo Hatfield**, Change Lead, Public Sector

'*The Inclusion Edge* is a page-turner. It had me eager to read on and get to the sections that challenged my thinking. It armed me with models and approaches to use and left me hungry to take action and do more as a leader in this space.'
— **Mark Blythe**, Global Operations Director, Airbnb

'I thoroughly enjoyed reading *The Inclusion Edge*. Every chapter provides you with different tools on how to tackle diversity and inclusion. I would have loved to have had this book when I started my career and would absolutely recommend everyone to read it.'
— **Besmira Tuga**, International Team Leader, FEXCO

'*The Inclusion Edge* is an excellent guide for leaders that find themselves navigating the new normal of needing to build a sustainable business through the lens of diversity, equity and inclusion. Mary's thirty plus years of experience in change management and organisational effectiveness are translated into a set of milestones that carve out a path for leaders to tailor and follow. *The Inclusion Edge* is a guide for right now!'
— **Colin Daley**, Senior Global Advisor, International Finance Corporation

THE
INCLUSION
EDGE

Confidently create a
culture that celebrates
diversity and belonging

MARY MCGUIRE

Re think

For Bernie, my first diversity teacher

Contents

Foreword

The world of work is always changing, and has altered significantly in the last few years. Innovation, societal shifts and many other factors contribute to this, and it is arguably what makes our workplaces so exciting. Imagine if your younger self turned up on your first day of work to be told that this was how it would be for the next forty plus years. You might get promoted but if there is no change, there is no opportunity to grow as a colleague and employee.

Sectors rise up rapidly and lose relevance just as quickly. Traditional ways of working, and the protocols that accompanied them, are mostly gone. Younger colleagues are aghast when I tell them that at one of my previous jobs, women were not allowed to wear trousers. I say we were not allowed to, but it was more of an unspoken rule, existing in a male-dominated workplace. As women were in the minority, it never occurred to us that we could question this.

The last few years have shown that the status quo can change within a fleeting period of time. They have given us the opportunity to re-evaluate how we see work and the change we can make as individuals. VUCA is a management acronym that has gained a huge amount of traction because it seems apt for how we view our world. It is short for volatility, uncertainty, complexity and ambiguity. If it is hard for a business to negotiate the issues around VUCA, what chance do individuals have? With no precedents to follow, how do you create a work ethos that can manage the many challenges and variations that come with VUCA? How do you manage 'known unknowns' in the absence of a culture that embraces experimentation, a culture that can only exist if colleagues feel that they are allowed to try and fail? Do you have the information and ability to deal with uncertainty? Do you encourage the sharing of that information, so that those silos that stop a full circle of capability cease to exist?

In asking all these questions, we must acknowledge that it is the collective effort of all the individuals who work within a company that equips us to handle VUCA. In creating a workplace where everyone feels valued and that they belong, we unleash power. The power of people who do not spend a huge amount of effort trying to fit in, but put that effort into creating a cohesive and collaborative workplace. The power to ask the tough questions that can push you forward but who ask in such a way that it is not seen as a challenge, but part of the way you work. A way of work that welcomes different voices, faces, experience and attitudes because the richer your mix is, the more influences can be brought to the discussion to help find new ways of solving problems.

Creating this rich mix is tough. If we are to have our own version of *Avengers Assemble* (forgive me, but I do work in cinema) with a cast of different characters who have their own individual talents, what do we need to do? In discussions that try to address this, some common themes appear. One of the barriers is that companies confuse policies with action. They assume that having a policy that says it is designed to drive inclusion will create inclusion. All too often, these policies are viewed as a tick-box exercise from human resources that can be safely skirted.

Certain elements of the workforce are not cognisant of the benefits of a diverse and inclusive personnel and treat it as a threat to their position or prospects. They see it as them getting a smaller slice of the pie, when all the evidence says the pie gets bigger with greater diversity. Other colleagues want to help drive change but do not know how and are concerned they will do the wrong thing. This creates two drag factors that need to speed up if we are to maintain the momentum of meaningful change; two more brakes on a process that is trying to address a complex issue that can appear intractable and deeply embedded in everything that we do. Anyone who thinks this can be changed by having a Pride week but not policies, International Women's Day without examining their gender pay gap, is indulging in a delusion.

For change to be fully embedded, we need to have allies in every seat. Individuals who know how to create cultures that foster inclusivity and belonging, and who can create a workplace where everyone can contribute and not feel the need to be someone or something that they aren't. In *The Inclusion Edge*, Mary has given the reader tools and tactics that help them become that change.

It can be hard to admit that you need support, but *The Inclusion Edge* can and will help you. It's inevitable that you'll make a mistake on your journey. That human fallibility is a key part of the process. If you take a deep breath and keep going, you will probably decide that any actions you didn't get right, or the moment when you realised a situation was more complex than you had anticipated, are your pivots of change. In trying to create a great environment for all your colleagues, by talking to them about how you can make them feel that they belong, you'll make a series of discoveries that will turn those issues into small obstacles in your journey towards a truly inclusive workplace.

Kathryn Jacob OBE
CEO of Pearl & Dean,
Co-Author of *Belonging* and *The Glass Wall*

Introduction

A business imperative that is impossible for leaders to ignore is the growing need to be aware of, sensitive to and able to champion diversity, equity and inclusion (DE&I). The global pandemic of 2020 and 2021 has, if anything, intensified this need. As Kathryn Jacob highlights in her foreword, we live in VUCA times, when our competitive environment and the needs of our employers and consumers have changed out of all recognition. The traditional ways of working are no longer viable and we need to carve a new path, one that is inclusive and enriched with diversity. This has been underlined by recent campaigns such as the #MeToo movement, which exposed widespread sexism in the entertainment industry, and the #BlackLivesMatter campaign, which exposed the gross injustice of police treatment towards black people in America after the death of George Floyd.

If you are a business leader, even with a good awareness of the issues facing diverse and minority groups, the area can feel like a minefield. If you have not been exposed to the issues facing those who are disadvantaged through gender, race, religion, sexuality and disability, it can feel overwhelming and as if it is best left to others to deal with. The reality is: the only person who can make a real and lasting change in the areas of DE&I in your business is you.

Who is *The Inclusion Edge* for?

I bring over thirty years of leadership and business advisory experience, having worked with corporations around the world on their thorny transformation and change agendas, and nothing is more challenging than DE&I. There is a gulf between the organisational intent and the leader's reality. How can you champion something you have no direct experience of? Leaders are frozen into inaction, feeling they should be doing something but not knowing what to do and somehow feeling responsible for the inequality that they are being asked to address.

This is no way to make inroads into the subject and is likely to make the gulf wider between what is intended and what is achieved, so how do you start? What if you make yourself vulnerable to ridicule? How do you shift from being a leader who is comfortable delegating tasks to one that will share personal and perhaps traumatic details about your life? How can you lead on something when it feels like you are the bad guy (and I do mean guy in this instance) because you represent the group that holds most power and influence, or it feels like your views and abilities are losing currency because you are not in an identified minority group?

If these questions resonate with you, you are not alone. Despite billions of pounds being spent on DE&I in organisations globally, the benefits are slow to trickle down beyond the platitudes shared in glossy annual reports. What organisation would not claim to be in support of DE&I these days? That does not make it any easier to implement as a business leader with competing priorities, performance targets to meet and precious little time to connect with people on anything more than a cursory level.

The Inclusion Edge builds on the ideas shared in my second book, *The Female Edge*. It has been designed with busy business leaders in mind. It is for those who want to do the right thing when it comes to building diverse teams and inclusive cultures, but are unsure where to start. Big teams, small teams, local teams or global teams; no matter the size of your employee population, *The Inclusion Edge* will guide you through a process of making your workplace more inclusive and increasing the sense of belonging. I am convinced that leaders can navigate this tricky path towards creating a culture of inclusion and belonging for all their people when they become aware of and willing to address the inequalities that exist. Most organisations will already have an extensive range of initiatives and activities to support their DE&I goals. This is a great start, but they are only springboards from which you, as a leader, must take your steer and walk your own path. Your people will look to you before any HR representative or well-formed DE&I statement to see what the reality is of inclusion in your workplace. If you have waited in the wings for DE&I to emerge fully formed in your business area or for someone to lead the way, then now is the time to stop waiting and start acting.

The six-step BELONG model

At the heart of any business is people: their stories, their beliefs, their identities and ultimately, their need to belong. You could be the person who makes that possible in your organisation, and *The Inclusion Edge* will help you to do this. It is based on a six-step process called the BELONG model, which will show you how:

- **B**ias awareness can open your eyes to the many ways inequality exists in society

- Embodying the values of belonging will enrich your life and make significant cultural shifts in your organisation

- Leveraging your own experience of exclusion will increase your empathy towards those who live with these experiences throughout their lives

- Open and curious behaviours lead to a deeper and richer understanding of your employees

- Nourishing green shoots of inclusion and belonging leads to increased team and business performance

- Growing opportunities for minorities creates diverse and enriched businesses that are more sustainable and more resilient to a volatile competitive environment

By following this model, you will go on a journey of self-discovery and self-education, and learn how to open yourself up to others so you are receptive to and aware of the needs of your people. People from different backgrounds and experiences working together to achieve a shared goal in mutual respect of each other's skills is at the heart of DE&I.

You can read this book all in one sitting, or dip in and out as you think best. Each chapter is short, written in plain English and with a summary section that provides clear and practical actions. You will find case studies throughout (all of the names have been changed). You can take all six steps of the BELONG model together or go through each one at your own pace. I will be your guide on this journey of self-discovery, drawing on my extensive experience – both professional and personal.

My own background

I come at the subject of DE&I from my own unique perspective. I was brought up in a working-class home in the UK, with a sister who had learning disabilities and autism, an alcoholic father and an anxious mother. I left school with no qualifications, no prospects and little clue what I was going to do with my life. Knowing that my circumstances would hold me in this limited place, I left my childhood city of Birmingham. Through hotel work I found the love of my life and settled down, becoming qualified in social work and, later, as a business consultant.

There are many experiences from growing up in this inner-city chaos that helped me to empathise with people from lower socio-economic backgrounds and show understanding of issues around disability. My biggest experience of exclusion, and one that helped me to understand the size of the issue for countless people, was when I lost my home and my job through coming out as a lesbian in the late 1980s. This was a time when there was little tolerance around same-sex relationships and losing your job because you were gay was not uncommon. Since then, I have experienced the typical sexism that most women recognise when they are in male-dominated industries.

These lived experiences inform and colour my views of the world of DE&I, and spur me on to help leaders around the world to become more inclusive and sensitive to the needs of others. Most leaders want to do the right thing, to inspire and develop their people and achieve outstanding results through cooperation. They just don't always know how to do it.

Through my career I have had the privilege of working with some outstanding leaders. My approach is simple: when we strip everything else away – power, status, role, religion, sexual identity – we are people who want to be valued, heard and understood. While the habits and behaviours involved in achieving this may feel challenging, those goals are not difficult to attain. It's surprising how little practice it takes to become competent in making deep connections with others.

Let me take you on a journey of self-discovery which promises to give you more than it takes away by showing you how to build a culture of belonging in your organisation and reap the many rewards that come with it. *The Inclusion Edge* is a book you can revisit time and again and find something new and inspiring to help you to be the inclusive leader you wish to be.

PART ONE

LAYING THE GROUNDWORK FOR CHANGE

1

Why Do You Need
An Inclusion Edge?

Before any journey of discovery or development, it is important to consider 'Why bother?' Given that time and energy are needed to learn a new subject, practise new skills and create new ways of working, we must ask ourselves, 'What's in it for me and is it worth the investment I am about to make?'

To a certain extent, you will have addressed these questions in your subconscious long before you picked up this book, but it is still useful to ask yourself, 'Why now?' While you are pondering this, let me share with you why inclusion makes sense from a business perspective. What is it about a greater investment in diversity, equity, inclusion and belonging that will be worthwhile for you and your business?

You don't have to look far to find research that shows a strong link between diversity and higher performance. Just as a cake recipe needs a variety of ingredients to make it interesting and edible, so in business we need a wide range of voices and ideas to innovate and grow. There are many reasons for this, but the most obvious one is that if we rely solely on old, outdated ideas and modes of thinking without bringing fresh energy and insights, we get left behind. We are no longer relevant to our customers or chosen market and we lack ways to refresh our products and services. Blackberry, Kodak and even Royal Bank of Scotland are all firms that looked too big to fail, and are now echo chambers of the power they once held. Top-down, hierarchical cultures that were the antithesis of belonging and relied on maverick leaders who behaved with arrogance and hubris caused the failure of these monoliths of the business world.[1]

When we become comfortable in our ways of working and performance seems good, much as it did to these giants of their industries, the idea of bringing diversity of thought, people and processes can feel challenging. Much like the effort it would take to go to the gym after many years of a sedentary lifestyle, the idea of doing something different can feel exhausting; but doing nothing is no longer an option if you want to stay current, credible and profitable. Not only is society changing, but the geo-economic ground of global business is also shifting and the expectations of you as a business leader have never been higher.

Relying on outmoded methods of leadership will no longer give you the edge. Being surrounded by people whose frame of reference is similar to yours from the perspective of culture, gender, race and religion will not cut it in modern business. You are in danger of becoming dated and irrelevant unless you face the challenges that are at your door. Kathryn Jacob et al explain the dynamic between old and new ways of interacting in their book, *Belonging*: 'Just as old-fashioned traditional culture is kept alive by thousands of tiny acts of exclusion and alienation of those who are different from the supposed norm, then a new positive culture of belonging will be created from everyday actions and positive affirmations of inclusivity.'[2]

The Inclusion Edge has been written with you, as a leader, in mind. While we will go through some challenging terrain and face some uncomfortable truths, we will also look at the many ways you can embrace DE&I authentically and wholeheartedly. By starting with the foundations, you will see that your unique experiences, including the challenges and difficulties that you have overcome in life, are your superfuel in learning to be open to and a visible champion of diversity and belonging.

The terminology explained

I will use the terms diversity, equity and inclusion as shorthand throughout the book, but there is a fourth key aspect of any diversity programme: belonging. Let's clarify our understanding of the terminology.

Diversity

This is the range of employees that make up your workforce. Diversity can have many dimensions, but will include gender, race, sexual orientation or identity, religion, disability or being differently abled, mental health challenges and neurodiversity at the least. Some employees might have one diverse trait, but it is not unusual for an individual to have many in what is called 'intersectionality', such as a black woman who identifies as lesbian and is a wheelchair user.

Equity

Equity is about equalising the field in terms of opportunity. By addressing the structural imbalance in our society, equity systematically unblocks inequalities. Typical examples can be found in the expectations within recruitment processes. If your jobs insist on 'red brick' (UK) or 'Ivy League' (USA) university graduates, then you are creaming off the top of an already elite pool. If you ask candidates to lift a minimum weight (typically 56 lbs) during selection for manufacturing roles when almost all heavy lifting is done by machines, or insist on a college degree for a relatively unskilled entry-level job, you are favouring some and discriminating against others. College degrees are still a path only open to those with the privilege of a stable home life and financial support. They do not reflect raw talent and ability, which can be found in many unqualified, yet enthusiastic candidates. If we continue to uphold the structural inequalities of society, we are doing little to shift the needle in terms of diversity and representation. Equity is about understanding we need to widen our net of search sources when we are hiring. We need to address the barriers head on and, if necessary, provide support and guidance to help diverse candidates to overcome them. Equity is about dismantling barriers, processes and systems that favour the few over the many.

Inclusion

To be inclusive as an organisation requires effort, investment and, above all, intention. Beyond attracting diverse talent, organisations need to address aspects of our culture and ways of working that may be unwelcoming and even alien to people from other cultures or backgrounds. Diversity without inclusion results in high levels of turnover from newly landed diverse staff, as they enter a culture that is not accepting or welcoming of them for who they are. Inclusion is building a culture that acknowledges and celebrates difference rather than dumbing it down. It finds a way to talk about why people see things in a different way and for them to share their experiences and world views in an open and receptive environment.

Belonging

If you are a parent who loves your children, then you know what belonging is. It is the unconditional acceptance of who they are and what they do, even if it differs vastly from who you are and what you do. Belonging in the workplace is similar. It is about embracing the differences both seen and unseen of your colleagues and accepting them for who they are.

How diversity benefits business

There are many studies that have seen a positive link between diversity and performance. You may have heard of the term 'groupthink', the tendency for a group to shortcut its thinking to the dominant or expected response. Carol Fulp argues that the lack of diversity in business often blinds leaders to the competitive realities and leads to misjudgements.[3] This is a likely outcome whenever teams lack diversity. The same questions will be raised and the same answers offered if everyone uses the same frame of reference. It is only by bringing in new and fresh thinking that we can break the status quo and allow innovation to shine through.

An increasingly global, interconnected business must embrace the diversity of its employees, its suppliers and its community. Not only is this good for business, it has a positive impact on wider society. In their 2018 report, *Delivering Through Diversity*, global management consultants McKinsey and Company found: 'Organizations that embrace best practices for creating a diverse workforce have achieved 28% higher revenue, doubled their net income and earned 30% high profits. Companies with the most ethnically diverse executive teams are 33% more likely to outperform peers in terms of profitability.'[4] In 2016, the UK government's McGregor-Smith Review on race in the workplace reported: 'If BME [black and minority ethnic] talent is fully utilised, the economy could receive a £24 billion boost.'[5]

There is a lot of hard evidence on the value that diversity brings to business performance. Quite apart from the business argument, there is a moral dimension. We know in our bones that treating people with respect and valuing their skills and experience leads to better performance. We only need to extend that thought to consider that, when harnessed and nurtured, the broad spectrum of humanity on this earth brings countless benefits in terms of team cohesion, increased knowledge, innovation and performance.

The question that remains is not why bother with diversity, but how can we afford not to? What are the business losses that we are making by not harnessing diversity and fostering inclusion? Are you ready to grow your business in a more sustainable and ethical way, not only because the data tells you it is right, but to build a culture your employees are proud to be involved in and want to actively support? Diversity is good for business, but this is not enough in and of itself to make a difference. We need to move from an appreciation of the business case into clear intentions.

Whose responsibility is it?

Now we have established a case for DE&I, the next question is whose responsibility is it? In a large and complex matrixed organisation, there are many over-lapping and sometimes competing priorities and initiatives and DE&I is just one among many. Who should lead on it, given that there are other targets and challenging business goals to meet?

Organisations often lean heavily on their HR or talent team to do the heavy lifting of DE&I and both have an important role to play. They are usually the backbone of DE&I in terms of policies, systems and processes. As a leader, it would be difficult to make progress without the support of HR, but supporting and leading are two different things. HR is there to provide the right conditions for DE&I to flourish, but it is the business leaders that make it happen. Employees' expectations are shaped by HR and the processes and systems of your organisation, but their experiences are defined by you – their boss and their senior leader. Instinctively, employees will look up to you to take direction and read the signs. Their direct experience at work is defined by what you ask them to do, by how you choose to behave, by what you say is acceptable and what is not.

DE&I is central to your leadership challenge. Are you a leader who is concerned with getting the best performance out of your people and creating a workplace where people thrive? If so, you can only do this by being a leader who takes time to get to know your employees and motivates them to do their best. A leader's role is about getting things done through others. You are only adding value to your organisation if you are managing this to the best of your ability. Your one role, perhaps your only role, is to know your people and to ensure that their tasks match their talents and that they are supported to deliver with encouragement and pride.

All of this is only possible if we create an environment where the whole person is acknowledged and welcomed. If we dumb down the person, merely treating them as a unit of production to get things done, it reduces employees to a transactional relationship in which only the trade of skills for money is important. We lose their inherent brilliance and creativity, for want of a bit more humanity in the way they are treated.

At the heart of DE&I is people, with all their foibles, eccentricities, beliefs and ways of behaving. You do not need to understand or even agree with these differences, but to get the best out of people, you need to respect them. Even though diversity is complex when we consider race, gender, religion, disability, mental health and sexual identity, at the core we are still people, coming together from different experiences and trying to cooperate to achieve a shared goal. Your job as a leader is to know your people, understand what motivates them and then create the environment that does that. Command-and-control leadership once believed that if we treated everyone equally and created a meritocracy where people thrived based on merit, then all would be well. The world has evolved beyond this view. We can no longer expect people to fit into a work role and leave the rest of themselves at home.

We also know that meritocracy, while laudable in its goals, forgets that not everyone can compete equally on a playing field that has been tilted towards some, while ignoring the needs of many. Equity has become a central component of diversity work by acknowledging that there are many barriers that restrict the ability for some to compete in the same way or at the same level, because they were never admitted to the institutions of influence or given the opportunities to do so.

Beyond your job title, your concerns and your priorities, your people will want to know you, the human who stands behind all of that, warts and all. When you show them that, and signal to them that they can do the same, magic happens. A collective sigh of relief can be heard as your employees understand they can leave behind all the protective layers that have made them skittish and uncooperative and can get on with doing a great job.

DE&I should not exist in a vacuum and will often be part of a multipronged strategy rolled out by HR and endorsed by the CEO. If you are wondering where to start, find out about your organisation's DE&I strategy. What are the priorities and what activities are planned throughout the year? There will be some great content you can use in meetings. Even promoting the strategy and the activities that are scheduled will signal to your team that you are making this a priority and taking it seriously.

There will undoubtedly be a leader training programme, which, if you have not done so yet, should be put on your priority list. This is likely to address areas such as unconscious bias, micro-aggressions or inclusive hiring. Take the time, do the work. Look around to get inspiration from your fellow leaders. Is there a senior leader who is regularly sponsoring activities or posting about diversity issues? Make a point of learning from them. If appropriate, ask them if they will be a light-touch mentor who can guide and support you as you go on this journey.

When you are more confident, you can start sponsoring activities and events in your team and your area. This could be at whatever level feels right for you. It might be a local community activity or part of a global programme, but your action and your support will be important. The BELONG model outlined in Chapter 4 gives you a framework for action. Based on practical experience, it is designed to take you through the process of becoming a confident, visible and consistent champion for DE&I.

Beyond a zero-sum mentality

One of the biggest impediments to making DE&I stick in most organisations is that it is perceived as a threat by those who hold power. In business, that is overwhelmingly white, male, heterosexual leaders. Diversity talks about everybody except those people, so if you are in that category it can feel like you no longer matter and that you are becoming irrelevant. This leads to an unhealthy stalemate in a business which is paying lip service to the issues facing minority groups. We need to reframe this. The difficulty with this either/or mentality is that we assume it is a zero-sum game. If I win you lose; if you win I lose. This sets us up to be competitive and combative towards each other and prevents us from building bridges of understanding.

We cannot ignore the real sense of threat of being publicly shamed or undermined as a white male leader, which leads to inaction, silence and resentment. One study by the Center for Talent Innovation (now Coqual) found that: 'A ripple of executive resignations and negative press in the summer of 2020 demonstrates the risk of getting D&I wrong. CrossFit, Starbucks and Bon Appétit were all brands that in 2020 paid the penalty for entrenched culture of bias or the actions of their leader.'[6] The truth is that if you are a majority leader, you have privileges and opportunities that others do not have. You can choose to hoard and defend these, or you can acknowledge they exist and see how you can help other people to find their success by supporting and encouraging them. There is enough opportunity to go around. There is enough respect and love to go around. We just need to be prepared to share it. This might mean holding on to your power a little less tightly and sharing that with others, so that they can thrive. As the saying goes, 'We can only give away what we have and by giving it away, it grows.'

The evolution of diversity, equity and inclusion

Terminology is one thing that trips up many leaders and it's not surprising since it is changing constantly. Terms that were common parlance even five years ago might now be frowned upon. The opportunity to put your foot well and truly in it is writ large in this arena, but there are ways you can become more astute and aware of what is going on and how things are changing.

Beyond the changing language, there is a fundamental truth at the heart of all DE&I activities: real barriers exist for certain groups in society and only with heightened awareness of those barriers and the will to dismantle them will change happen. Breaking down these barriers is the work of the many, not the few, and those of us who are in the position of privilege need to be part of the solution. People will forgive you for not using the correct term in how you have addressed a sector of diversity, but they will not forgive you for standing on the sidelines and doing nothing.

In earlier iterations of DE&I, the focus was on positive discrimination; giving someone from a diverse background a chance at a role based on potential. This was not well received, least of all by the diverse employee, who was often treated with a fair degree of patronisation by the hiring organisation and with disparity by their co-workers for having standards 'lowered' to get in. The quota system was favoured, where set targets across mainly race and gender were defined. This was seen by almost everyone as a tick-box exercise and positive discrimination is still a phrase used to describe DE&I today. Once the quota was met, the diverse employee was left navigating what was often a hostile work environment, which often led to a high turnover of diverse staff who were treated poorly and unsupported.

DE&I is no longer about tokenism, where we bestowed charity on a person based on their diverse characteristic (usually gender or race). While there were some laudable achievements that came out of this, it had more than a hint of condescension: the privileged majority allowing in the underprivileged minorities.

In *The Inclusion Imperative*, Stephen Frost talks about the three stages of the evolution of DE&I. Diversity 1.0 was born from the period between the civil rights era of the 1960s and the 1990s discrimination bills, which focused on raising awareness through education and enforcement through quotas. Frost makes a case for using quotas, although places this firmly within the context of the ideal: 'The argument in favour of quotas, rarely well made, is actually quite succinct. If we assume that IQ and talent is equally split among the sexes, and we have no reason or evidence to suggest otherwise, then in an ideal world, power and decision making would be reflective of that talent.'[7]

Diversity 2.0 created inclusion programmes, celebrating differences yet still reliant on training such as unconscious bias or sponsorship programmes for under-represented groups. Frost argues that Inclusion 3.0, as he coins it, is about taking a human approach: 'Inclusion 3.0 starts from the premise that people want to do "the right thing", they just need some practical tools, rather than to be lectured at.'[8]

Modern thinking around DE&I has evolved. We still have data to capture and goals around representation to achieve, but they are goals, not quotas. Instead of positive discrimination, we talk about hiring from a 'diverse slate', which encourages recruiters to work harder to find candidates from diverse backgrounds, instead of fishing in the same small pond of talent. A positive development has been the rise of affinity groups or employee resource groups where like-minded employees can share their experience as a woman, a working parent or a black person, in a safe and supportive environment. Their voices can contribute to policy development and raise awareness across the organisation.

Summary

We know that DE&I is good for business, but knowledge on its own is not enough. It takes more than a rational awareness of the benefits to make change happen. In this chapter, we have set the scene for DE&I. We have covered the terminology that will be used, discussed the benefits and confirmed your responsibility as a leader to be front and centre of any strategy roll-out.

DE&I strategies have evolved over the last fifty years, and so must you. While data and goals are important, it is imperative to address the barriers that exist and provide meaningful support to minority groups. Equity is the process we use to break down those barriers and help to bring more diverse talent and expertise to our organisation, and reap the many benefits that DE&I promises.

At its heart, DE&I is a strategy for people. Creating a workplace where people feel they truly belong requires authenticity and psychological safety – a place where revealing important aspects of our lived experience will be honoured and respected rather than disparaged. As a leader, you need to step into your own vulnerability, recognise your own limitations and share your learning openly with others. This is the route to a culture of true belonging.

SUGGESTED EXERCISES

1. Write down your motivation for making DE&I one of your top priorities. Define what you see as the benefits and the challenges.

2. Where can you go for more support and information to help you with your intentions?

2

Three Uncomfortable Truths

We need to get the hard stuff out of the way early so we can concentrate on what to do about it. In this chapter, we will address the three big uncomfortable truths – the elephants in every room when we are talking DE&I. They are by no means the only ones, but these three will lead the way to see the many forms that inequality takes in society. It is going to be uncomfortable reading, but it's a bit like the sticking plaster – once we get it off, we can get on with the job of addressing what's underneath.

Our society is not equal. Not even close. Even if you treat everyone with respect and dignity and are considerate of their needs, that does not mean that this is how they experience the world. It just means that is how they experience your world. Many of us make the mistake of believing that how we interact with people across many sections of society reflects how society acts. This has the effect of diminishing the experiences of people who experience sexism, racism and homophobia on a daily basis.

Awareness that this is the reality for large sections of our society is a good starting point in becoming a more inclusive leader. All modern western society was built on conquest and subjugation. As uncomfortable as that is to hear, it is our truth. In our collective past we built power structures that favoured the few over the many, the powerful over the weak. Yes, we have evolved and become more tolerant, but we have not dismantled these structures. Even if we want to believe that our modern lifestyle and liberal views have changed things, little has changed for those who already had the privilege of power or being part of the dominant culture and, as a result, neither has it changed much for those who did not.

What are the three uncomfortable truths?

The three areas that are at the top of almost every organisation's agenda when they embark on a journey towards greater inclusivity are race, gender and LGBTQ+ communities, because we know from the data that they are poorly represented beyond a certain point in management. Even if they account for sizeable proportions of the community in which you operate, they are still likely to be under-represented in your organisation, particularly at the more senior levels.

We could say that this is mere coincidence, that you don't have the right brand or roles or pay to attract those people. Or maybe it is because how you are attracting people is by saying, 'Our people look like me, they sound like me and they think like me. It's not that people from diverse backgrounds are discouraged from applying for a role. Far from it, everyone can have a shot, but mostly it will come down to whether or not I like you.' This is the case for the majority of modern businesses. They are making efforts to become more diverse and representative but they are failing miserably. Tech giants such as Google and Facebook (now Meta) have been wrestling with these issues for years and even with big hitters like Sheryl Sandberg from Meta championing female equity, they are still only achieving 37% female representation across their entire employee populations.[9]

This is a fundamental schism in our society that will take considerable effort to right. The good news is that by raising your awareness of how these three key groups are poorly represented across your business and even in your immediate team, you can start to consider what to do about it. Let's take them each in turn.

Racism

Racism is a fact in all western society. It was built on imperialism, colonialism and slavery. The dominant forces were white and the subjugating nations were often people of colour or of an ethnic group that was so damaged it would now be seen as a minority. We are all standing on the shoulders of racists and we have inherited some of their legacy.

Racism plays out from the belief that there is a preferred and dominant race and that all others are subservient to it. The white Caucasian dominated and sought to control most other nations as they spread out of Europe into Asia, Africa, the Americas and Australasia. Through the work of colonists, missionaries and even slavers, the worlds of people from vastly different nations were turned upside down when the white man came.

In modern times, the outcomes for non-white races in the USA, UK, Australia and Europe are poor when compared to outcomes for white people. Outcomes such as economic status, wealth, housing, education, career and social standing are all likely to be lower based on the colour of your skin, and race continues to divide societies. The Black Lives Matter movement emerged from the growing racial divide in the USA and the unfair treatment that people of colour experience. These issues are not only experienced in America, but right across Europe and Australasia as well.

According to one UK-based study, the level of unemployment is disproportionately high for people of colour. The McGregor-Smith Review found the employment rate for BME groups is only 62.8% compared with an employment rate for white workers of 75.6%. This gap is even worse for some ethnic groups; for instance, the employment rate for those from a Pakistani or Bangladeshi background is only 54.9%.[10]

Research by the Chartered Institute of Personnel and Development found there is a significant lack of ethnic diversity at the top of UK organisations. Ethnic minority employees are more likely than those from a white British background to say they have experienced discrimination, that their career progression has failed to meet their expectations and that they have felt the need to change aspects of their behaviour to 'fit' into the workplace.[11] According to data collected by the US Equal Employment Opportunity Commission, on average US$112.7 million is lost by employers for racial discrimination violations each year.[12]

Housing is likely to be poorer and in less safe areas if you are a person of colour, an immigrant or a refugee, and the range of services and amenities around you will be considerably reduced. If you are black, you are not likely to receive the same level of justice if a crime is committed against you. A brutal and sad example of this was the Stephen Lawrence case.

Stephen Lawrence was eighteen years old, living in Eltham in South London in the family home, when he was killed in 1993, in a racist attack. The police in London were called to investigate the crime but closed the case due to lack of evidence. In the years that followed his murder, Stephen's parents kept fighting for justice for their son. Many people believed the police treated Stephen's case differently because he was black – and that some officers acted in a racist way. An inquiry into Stephen's killing and the police investigation was held, and in 1999 it found that the Metropolitan police were 'institutionally racist'. Racist attitudes and beliefs were seen as normal and affected how they investigated Stephen's murder.

Racism is a fact of our society. Many of the difficulties in our working environment come down to the denial that it exists. Individuals may say 'I treat everyone the same' or 'I don't even notice someone's colour', but that does not help, because that singular frame of reference does not play out in wider society and does much to dismiss something that is a reality for many.

A truly pivotal work on the subject of race is *White Fragility* by Robin DiAngelo. Herself a white educationalist of many years' experience, DiAngelo found that when teaching white people about race, their reactions were often defensive and/or minimised the effects of racism in society. White people deny the idea that they have privilege merely by being white. Of course, some white people are disadvantaged and live in poverty, but they still belong to a class that is overwhelmingly powerful, as DiAngelo illustrates:

'If, for example, we look at the racial breakdown of the people who control our institutions, we see telling numbers in 2016–2017:

- Ten richest Americans: 100 percent white (seven of whom are among the ten richest in the world)

- US Congress: 90 percent white

- US governors: 96 percent white

- Top military advisors: 100 percent white

- President and vice president: 100 percent white

- US House Freedom Caucus: 99 percent white

- Current US presidential cabinet: 91 percent white

- People who decide which TV shows we see: 93 percent white

- People who decide which books we read: 90 percent white

- People who decide which news is covered: 85 percent white

- People who decide which music is produced: 95 percent white

- People who directed the one hundred top-grossing films of all time, worldwide: 95 percent white

- Teachers: 82 percent white

- Full-time college professors: 84 percent white

- Owners of men's professional football teams: 97 percent white'[13]

If the main structures of power and influence (politics, business, media and entertainment) are dominated by white people, then we cannot deny that privilege must play a part.

Sexism

I wrote about the unequal treatment of women in my last book, *The Female Edge*. Gender inequality plays out in business, but the issue is far wider than that. Just as we have created a racist foundation for society through colonialism, imperialism and racial segregation, we have built our modern society on patriarchy – the view that men know best and can decide what society needs.

As with people of colour, the outcomes for women when compared to men are poor. Great strides have been made in this area and we have achieved things like a female prime minister, a female head of the European Central Bank, and many great business CEOs are women, but these achievements are in the minority. That we still have to talk about women as part of the diversity effort speaks volumes, given that they make up 51% of the population, have the same educational outcomes as men (and sometimes better) and, at least in the early career years, the same job experience. When we look beyond the first level of management, we see that women fall away in ever-increasing numbers until, as we reach the top levels of organisations, managers are almost exclusively male. If both genders start at the same place and time with similar abilities and skills, it begs the question, why would such a big disparity occur?

We do not have to go back far in society to find that women were expected to be quiet, genteel and wholly accepting of the dominance of men. In Victorian times, women were seen as unattractive if they were in any way analytical. Only 100 years ago, women were fighting and dying for the right to have a say in their country's politics. Fifty years ago, legislation for equal pay between men and women was introduced in the UK and the USA, and followed by many other countries, to combat the common practice of paying women less than men for the same role. Yet when the UK introduced gender pay gap reporting in 2017, it uncovered the widespread practice of differential pay continuing to favour men. In their book, *How Women Rise*, Helgesen and Goldsmith list 'sexist bosses', 'career tracks that assume families do not exist' and 'performance review criteria subtly designed to favour men' among the 'unconscious biases that shape hiring and promotion.'[14]

Organisations are hungry beasts that are constantly looking for the next big thing, the next big priority, the next big market. Their demands can be relentless, especially as you go further up the chain of command. This converts into long hours, lots of travel and endless meetings. It naturally favours someone who can be ever present and is able to change plans at the drop of a hat, which does not reflect the reality for many working women who often have the main caring responsibilities at home. This inherent bias in senior roles is reflected in the reality that men are rising to the top and women are being left behind, as Deloitte Global outline in their report, *Women in the Boardroom*: 'Although the percentage of women on boards inched closer to 20%, there are comparatively few female board chairs (6.7% now, as compared to 5.3% in the previous edition). Female CEOs are even rarer, at 5% in 2021 and 4.4% in the previous edition.'[15] According to the 2021 study by McKinsey and Company, *Women in the Workplace*, women face 'a broken rung' at the bottom of the promotion ladder, which means that 'for every 100 men promoted to manager, only 86 women are promoted.'[16]

The Covid-19 pandemic was a serious disruptor of the workplace. When working from home became a necessity and global travel was stopped, businesses were forced to find new ways of working. On the face of it, this provided an opportunity to level the playing field as it stripped back the presenteeism and constant travel prevalent in some organisational cultures, but it did not help women that much in the end. Women continue to leave the workplace at a faster rate than men in the post-Covid new normal. A recent study by

Deloitte found that a major factor driving the Great Resignation included the 'lack of opportunities to advance and burnout rising to the top of the list of drivers for those who had left or were actively considering leaving their employers'.[17]

This does not bode well for the long-term situation of achieving gender equity in the workplace. If we continue to build organisations, career paths and jobs that are weighted towards a traditional model where men work and women have supporting roles, then we are failing both men and women. Both feel trapped in a system that is insensitive to the realities of family life.

Bias towards men as leaders prevails in our larger consciousness and we are still more likely to promote an incompetent man over a competent woman. In his book *Why Do So Many Incompetent Men Become Leaders?*,[18] Chamorro-Premuzic suggests that this is because we confuse confidence with competence. A man will say he can do a job because he is confident he will work out the nuances of the role, even if he has never done it before. A woman will say she can do a job if she is certain she is at least 90% competent to do so. These differing behaviours lead to very different outcomes – as gender representation in senior roles reflects.

Homophobia

The last of the three uncomfortable truths is how people who identify as LGBTQ+ are treated in the workplace. The definition of homophobia is dislike of or prejudice towards gay people. LGBTQ+ stands for lesbian, gay, bisexual, transgender, questioning or plus. The 'plus' represents other sexual identities not covered by the other five initials.

Less than sixty years ago in the UK, you could be defined as legal or illegal based on your sexual orientation. Homosexuality was a crime and many men (it was almost always men) ended up in prison because of who they loved. Perhaps one of the most poignant and ironic cases was of the famous code breaker, Alan Turing, who during World War II cracked what was believed to be an unbreakable German code. It was the sign of a brilliant analytical mind. As a result of his breakthrough, many important German commands were intercepted, which led to key military victories for the allied forces and was pivotal in bringing the war to an early conclusion.

That did not account for much in the eyes of the British public when Turing was tried and convicted for homosexual acts a few years after the war. He agreed to a treatment called chemical castration rather than face a prison term, and was dead two years later, possibly from suicide. Although a posthumous pardon was issued in 2013, together with a widespread pardon of all men convicted of homosexual acts in the past, the fear of retaliation based on sexual orientation is still prevalent.

More recently, there was a big debate in the UK in the early 2000s about same-sex marriage. There were powerful arguments against this on both sides of the political parties and in the religious groups stating that it would undermine the sanctity of marriage. The other recurring argument against allowing same-sex marriage was the concern that it would sully the young minds of future generations and turn them gay or make being gay more acceptable to them. The concern was that young minds are easily influenced and if allowed to see something as normal that is considered abnormal in the eyes of the majority, they would somehow choose it over what is right and expected of them. The same type of argument is sometimes used for any choice a child might make that differs from the expectations of their parents.

The final and perhaps most insidious argument was that if gay men married and were allowed to raise children (lesbians don't get off lightly but were seen in a more benign light) they were more likely to sexually abuse them. The overwhelming evidence of child sexual abuse in both girls and boys is that it is perpetrated by men who, on the face of it, follow a heterosexual lifestyle.

In 2005, the UK law was passed for civil partnerships between same-sex couples, and later extended to allow marriage. It is now fairly common in most western countries.

What does this mean for LGBTQ+ in the workplace? One of the biggest concerns for individuals is whether they can be fully out at work. Can they declare themselves as gay, introduce their partner at work events and will their status adversely affect their career ambitions? According to research by the University of California, employment discrimination against LGBT people in the form of 'being fired, not hired, or harassed because of their sexual orientation or gender identity' continues to be persistent and widespread, leading to the reality that,

> 'Over 40% of LGBT workers (45.5%) reported experiencing unfair treatment at work, including being fired, not hired, or harassed because of their sexual orientation or gender identity at some point in their lives. Many LGBT employees reported engaging in "covering" behaviours to avoid harassment or discrimination at work.'[19]

When you feel you must hide some aspect of your innate personality because it will be viewed negatively by others and may harm your career prospects, this is the opposite of belonging. For millions of people around the world, it is their living reality. They will often keep their sexual orientation or identity hidden, rather than risk the ridicule or judgement that might follow.

Recently, I was holding focus groups for a profes-sional services organisation when one man shared what happened when he landed his dream job in a previous organisation.

HOSTILITY FROM DAY ONE

On his first day in the role, my client introduced himself to the leadership team and shared details about his personal life and partner, which immediately signalled his sexual orientation. In the meeting, his boss said to him, 'I wouldn't have hired you if I knew you were a poof.' This casual disdain sent a message to the rest of the team that being anything other than heterosexual would not be tolerated. Needless to say, he did not stay around long to deal with such outright hostility.

Around 10% of your employees will be in the LGBTQ+ bracket. Some may be at the subtle end of questioning and not showing up on anyone's radar. Others will be either openly or obviously gay. Whether they choose to fully admit that will depend on their own experiences and how well your organisation signals that they will be accepted whoever they are and whatever their identity.

Why do we turn a blind eye to discrimination?

Looking at these three sectors of society and how they are treated makes for uncomfortable reading, but it is a necessary part of setting the stage for the work that we need to do going forward. We cannot achieve a culture of belonging if we have a skewed picture of society and we fail to see the realities for many minority groups. There are three main reasons why this happens in the majority of organisations.

Awareness

There is an old adage that says: 'What you cannot measure, you cannot manage.' The same is true for change. You cannot change what you are not aware of, so the first step in the process of change is becoming aware that a problem exists. Awareness in and of itself is not enough, but it is a crucial precursor to effective action. I applaud the many organisational initiatives that introduce unconscious bias training. I don't applaud the view that this is enough to change culture. If awareness was enough, we wouldn't have smokers or drug addicts. The fact is that our thinking never changes the world, but our actions do. Why do many leaders, when they become aware of the discrimination and barriers to advancement that exist, fail to do anything about it?

Time

According to Coqual: '[Majority Men] who haven't gotten involved in their companies' D&I efforts cited "I'm too busy" as the biggest hurdle... This is a fundamental challenge that people leaders face today: we need to move D&I off the sidelines and fully integrate it into the operating ethos of our organizations.'[20] Time is an argument that we all use for not doing something, because we have chosen to do something else in its stead. Often, the time argument is about our mental capacity to take on new ideas and behaviours, rather than the minutes and hours that would need to be invested in achieving something.

As we have seen, better DE&I leads to improved and sustainable business performance, and what could possibly be more important in achieving your objectives? Time, when used as an excuse to do nothing, often reflects a lack of intention to change the status quo, which results from low confidence and the fear factor of doing something wrong. Moving beyond these two barriers is the main objective of *The Inclusion Edge*.

Fear

The number one reason I see leaders doing the bare minimum for DE&I is not apathy but a fear of doing something wrong. The fear of putting your foot in it when you reach out to your employees, or support a cause that affects those from under-represented groups, is real and the backlash can be uncompromising. Coqual put this succinctly when they observe: 'It's jarring to be "called out" on an act of bias – or "hit a speed bump"… But silence, disengagement and defensiveness are poor short-term strategies that halt meaningful change towards a belonging culture.'[21] We have to get beyond fear to a place of openness and curiosity.

In the spirit of feeling the fear and doing it anyway, *The Inclusion Edge* is about unpacking the many aspects of DE&I and equipping you with tools and techniques to build your confidence and create meaningful dialogue with your under-represented employee groups. By tapping into your own exclusion experiences – and we all have at least one – and sharing these with honesty and humility, you will find that authentic dialogue opens up and leads to meaningful change.

Summary

In this chapter, we have looked at how and where modern society favours the few over the many, and in particular the three main constituents who receive unfavourable treatment. Racism, sexism and homophobia are strong in our history, and continue to feature despite all the civil rights and legal protections that have been created.

It is important to recognise that these issues exist, even if you have not been directly affected by them or known someone who has. Your own point of reference is not a valid litmus test on whether other people experience discrimination. You can't claim that it doesn't happen merely because you have not experienced discrimination yourself.

You can be a force for good in how you choose to set the tone and signal the sense of belonging you wish to create in your organisation. In the next chapter we will break down the steps you can follow to achieve positive and lasting change.

SUGGESTED EXERCISES

1. Educate yourself on either one or all of the issues highlighted in this chapter. There are many great books and films out there that can help you. Three I can recommend are:

   Gender: *The Authority Gap* by Mary Ann Sieghart (Black Swan, 2022)

   Race: *White Fragility* by Robin DiAngelo (Penguin, 2019)

   LGBTQ+: *GaYme Changer* by Jens Schadendorf (LID Publishing, 2021)

2. Choose one action you can take to support one of these populations and signal your willingness to be an ally or sponsor.

3
Where To Start

It can be difficult when you want to be more visible and supportive of DE&I, but genuinely don't know where to start, especially if you do not identify with an under-represented group or have no direct experience of discrimination. I encourage my clients to start with what they know. Most people have an experience to build upon, either from lived or self-taught insights into what it means to be on the outside of power, acceptance or opportunity.

Understanding seen and unseen differences

Your technical and leadership skills did not start with and will not end with your current organisation, and neither will your learning and upskilling in the field of DE&I. In the previous chapter, we looked at the three key sectors of society that are adversely affected in the workplace, but they are the tip of the iceberg. Diversity can come in many forms and often there are more unseen differences than seen.

The iceberg model was first introduced by Edward T Hall in his seminal book, *Beyond Culture*.[22] The analogy was that only a small amount of the differences are above the waterline and can be seen, whereas below the waterline there are many differences which will still be relevant and affecting culture that are not seen.

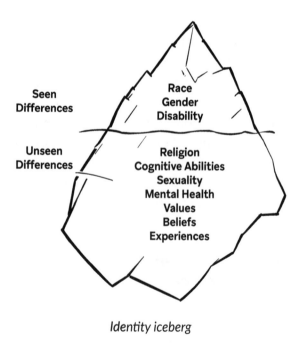

Identity iceberg

From a DE&I perspective, this model is helpful in considering the 'seen' differences above the water-line such as gender, race, disability and the 'unseen' differences below the waterline, such as religion, cognitive diversity, sexual orientation etc. It shows how wide-ranging diversity is and how, if we take it to its conclusion, everyone is diverse, since we all have unique facets of our identity.[23]

The idea of both seen and unseen differences is a good way to frame diversity in a much wider context. It is not just aspects of identity that can polarise society (such as gender, race, sexuality and disability), but more subtle traits such as political views, religious beliefs, languages and life experiences. Your first step in the journey is uncovering what already exists in and around your working life. That means looking within your own personal life experiences, but also among your employee population.

Based on the observable differences and even some of the unseen differences that you are aware of, map out the make-up of your immediate team and then look across your division and organisation. What does this tell you about diversity in your workplace? How easy is it for people to declare some of those aspects of their identity that are below the waterline? If you had to put a score between 1 (low) and 10 (high) on how well your culture encompasses belonging, what would that score be? Is there anything you can do to positively influence it? Find out about the experiences of those who grew up in a minority racial group, or who are on the autism spectrum, or who are gay at work. There are many sources that can help you. Some further reading was suggested at the end of the last chapter, and there are additional resources at the back of this book to help you to widen your perspective of diversity.

Perspective is everything

You have probably seen the dual-aspect picture which can be interpreted as either an old woman or a young woman. This famous optical illusion first appeared in 1888 on a German postcard and was adapted in 1915 by British cartoonist William Ely Hill under the title, *My Wife and My Mother-in-Law.*

Depending on the perspective you take, you will be drawn to one image over the other. Once you have imprinted the first image on your mind, it can be notoriously difficult to find the second image. This kind of fixed thinking happens when we have a one-sided perspective and are unwilling or unable to consider things from another viewpoint. Just put this picture in front of a group of students who have never seen it before and see what happens.

We could probably put all the conflicts in the world down to two things: different belief systems, which influence our perspective, or seeking more power. Modern society is built on conquest: dominance and submission; victory and defeat; power and powerless. These inequalities are hardwired into how we have built modern societies. We no longer have widespread slavery, women are not excluded from political life and we do not have state-backed religious persecution, yet the effects of these historical events still echo in our current reality.

Religious strife often comes down to different belief systems. How I view my god and how I worship them, is different to how you view and worship your god. We don't allow or encourage religious discussions at work (unless of course we are a belief-based organisation) but the thinking that leads to religious intolerance is rooted in this lack of understanding. Cultures that do not allow for any level of dissent, where leaders prohibit their employees from questioning their motives or where freedom to express different opinions is not allowed, are playing out the same level of intolerance but in a nonsecular environment.

When we seek the higher moral ground to justify our view of the world as the right one, we are by default saying that everyone else is in the wrong. In religious and ethnic strife (ethnic differences are two people from the same racial group but with differing belief and cultural systems), whether you belong and are accepted depends on how well you conform to the dominant belief system. Those outside of these shared beliefs are shunned.

If we apply those same behavioural traits to how we run organisations, and replace religious ideologies with leadership expectations, we can see how command-and-control cultures create a similar dynamic. We create a culture of patronage (access to power and influence) that is based on bestowing privilege on some and shunning others. Some organisations believe that this is how you create a high-performing culture. Despite all evidence to the contrary, a surprising number still hold on to these outmoded and ineffective models of leadership.

Vibrant societies are those that go beyond tolerance to celebrating differences and using them as a source of inspiration, curiosity and discovery. Outstanding insights, ways of working and achievements emerge that would have been impossible from a monoculture. The same is true in open and curious organisations.

Finding common ground

One way we can overcome some of these hardwired responses to difference is to deal with them head on. Bringing to the surface what is not discussed or what is feared will help to uncover outmoded ways of thinking and build bridges to understanding.

In their busyness, many organisations are poor at allowing this space to help different groups understand each other and how they see the world. It is viewed as frivolous or time-wasting, and it sometimes seems impossible to take time to reflect and talk due to work pressures. The cost of not creating this space is far greater, creating an unseen drag that slows everything down. Communication is more cumbersome, meetings take longer and important instructions get misinterpreted. Not paving the way to find common ground leads to poor performance and the law of diminishing returns.

Beyond belief systems, work ethics, food choices and traditions, we find universal human wants and needs. Everyone wants a life where they have a safe place to live, where they can put food on the table for themselves and their family, where they can find well-paid work where their contribution is valued and their opinions are heard. In 1943 Abraham Maslow summarised that common ground beautifully in his hierarchy of needs framework, which remains one of the most respected models of human motivation.[24]

Maslow explained that our actions are motivated by needs that rise in importance, based on our ability to fulfil them. It is not possible to fulfil the higher-level needs of achieving one's potential if we do not have our basic needs of food and shelter met. This is why it is represented by a pyramid of needs, with the most basic needs at the bottom and the more complex needs at the top.

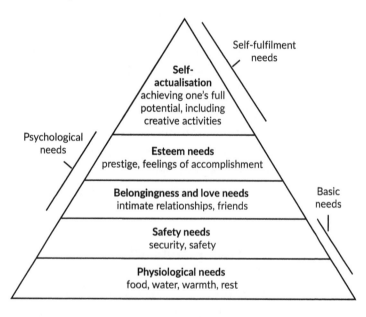

Maslow's hierarchy of needs[24]

It may seem obvious, but we are all striving for the same peak – to live our life in a way that allows us to express our truth, achieve our goals and look after our loved ones. Finding common ground starts with appreciating that as human beings we have more that binds us than sets up apart. We are social beings that have evolved across geographic, racial, ethnic and belief boundaries. We have created large, complex societies that have learned to transcend our tribal heritage.

Businesses are a great place to build common ground, even if outside their walls there is a lot of strife. In Northern Ireland during the troubles of the 1970s and 1980s, ethnic divisions ran along religious or patriotic lines. You were either Catholic or Protestant. Loyalist or Nationalist. Tensions were high between the groups and often spilled out into violence in the streets and terrorist campaigns. Despite this backdrop, many businesses and employers found a way to create common ground. They employed people from across the sectarian divides and put them together working on the same shop floor or in the same teams. Whatever differences existed were left at the door, because when people came to work they had a job to do and their value was in their role and their skills.

How can you build common purpose among your teams, especially if they come from different cultures and backgrounds? It starts with conversation and simple curiosity. I have seen this done well in technology businesses that use a simple format called 'fireside chats' to bring leaders and guests in to talk about their experience and take questions. Even the term 'fireside' engenders the concept of a relaxed and cosy chat, echoing a time when our primal ancestors would sit around the campfire swapping stories. Another format I have seen that works well is lunch-and-learn, or care-to-share, where a different food or cultural event is celebrated and someone who perhaps comes from that culture explains its history and traditions.

A simpler method I have used when bringing new teams together, especially when they come from and are working in different parts of the world, is to take time in our early sessions to share our personal histories. Not in any long, drawn-out way but just inviting each individual to 'Tell us about yourself.' Taking time at the start of creating a new team for each person to get to know their colleagues brings countless benefits. They see themselves as a team who understand each other and value listening and respecting each other's background, and they know that their leader is interested in them. Perhaps most important of all, they have a model they can take back to their respective teams and replicate.

Summary

A big part of your DE&I journey is knowing where to start in an area that can feel overwhelming and fraught with difficulties. In this chapter, we have looked at some of the ways you can overcome this: for example, by building common ground and getting beyond the fear factor. Using the identity iceberg and Maslow's hierarchy of needs helps to see people in the round and not as a set of labels. When you build common ground among your teams, they learn to look beyond differences and see areas of cooperation and shared objectives.

SUGGESTED EXERCISES

1. Look deeper into your immediate family and network of friends to see if you can identify examples of under-represented identities.
   If appropriate, ask these people about their experiences and how they address barriers they have faced.

2. Look at the data of your teams, including everyone who reports to you. What can you see about the make-up of each team in terms of gender, race, disability (if known), sexuality (if known) and whether there is a disparity between the top and the bottom of your reporting line?

3. Reflect on what biases or barriers might have existed to create your current team profile.

PART TWO

THE BELONG MODEL – SIX STEPS TO CREATING A CULTURE THAT CELEBRATES DIVERSITY AND INCLUSION

4
The BELONG Model: A Framework For Action

To confidently create a culture of diversity and belonging you first need to become aware and then, through that awareness, do something about what you know. Many organisations focus on the first step and raise consciousness of the many issues that face minority groups, but then leave it there and hope that action will follow. If the last sixty years of civil rights campaigns have taught us anything, it is that awareness, while crucial to change, is not in itself the end goal.

Change happens through action, and positive change happens through informed and mindful awareness. That is why I created the BELONG model, to give you a roadmap for change.

The BELONG model

I use the journey metaphor a lot in my work, as I see all change as a step-by-step process. There are six steps to take in our journey to creating a culture that celebrates diversity and belonging.

Step One: Bias awareness

We cannot change what we are not aware of. That is true for every change we want to make in life. To become an inclusive leader, the first step is awareness. It is through this awareness that we understand the gaps in our knowledge and can do something about them.

Noticing bias inherent in society highlights what you don't know but are now aware of. A lot of the kickback from DE&I programmes comes from the view that what a person sees and what they understand mirrors the world that they live in. If they don't see discrimination or bias and don't believe they act from it themself, it does not exist. This leads to resistance to get involved or actively lead DE&I in business because it is viewed as irrelevant, but as we covered in Chapter 1, DE&I is not only becoming a business imperative, it is good for business as well.

Noticing bias in yourself, your organisation and among your colleagues and employees will help you take the next step.

Step Two: Embody belonging

Your organisation probably has a set of values that are shared widely internally and externally to say how and why they do things the way they do. It is worth asking how well these values overlap with your own. Have you ever sat down and looked at your own values? If you haven't, we'll cover this in Chapter 6.

Are your and your organisation's values consistent with the values of belonging? What are the values of belonging? Are they values you can identify with and act on? These are deep questions, but to lead confidently in the DE&I space, you need to do the inner work and that includes uncovering, owning and sharing your values. Not only will it help if you have an internal compass to guide your actions in any situation, but it will allow you to speak more eloquently about your reasons for embracing DE&I. This is critical for the next step: building bridges of connection through personal disclosure.

Step Three: Leverage experience

When shared sensitively, your own experiences of exclusion will help you to build bridges with your under-represented employees. Connection comes through shared experiences and understanding. I have yet to find a person who has not suffered some kind of exclusion or lack of belonging in their life. The impact on your life may have been much less dramatic than for some of your employees, but these experiences will still convey your awareness and show empathy.

Step Four: Open and curious

From a place of awareness, we can deepen our understanding of our employees' stories. What have they been through? Why do they see the world the way they do? What would help them perform even better? Through your questions and curiosity you will learn some amazing things about your colleagues.

How and when you ask these questions is crucial, and in Chapter 8 we will go through the many ways you can become more open and curious without causing offence.

Step Five: Nourish green shoots

Nourishing green shoots of change comes from being alert to the opportunities that exist all around you. You can become aware of new and interesting initiatives in your direct team, in your wider organisation or in the local community. Your influence as a leader can play a significant role in whether or not something is successful, so by actively taking up activities in support of minority groups you are sending strong signals about your intent.

Step Six: Grow opportunities

The last step of the BELONG model is growing opportunities for minorities. This may be within the context of what is already happening in your organisation, or it may be something that you can create in your area. There are many levers that you can pull to help minority groups, from how you recruit and the activities that you develop within your teams, to the decisions you make about organisations you partner with to fulfil your requirements. By being more aware of the opportunities within your own sphere of influence and using them consciously, you will send powerful messages of support to the DE&I cause.

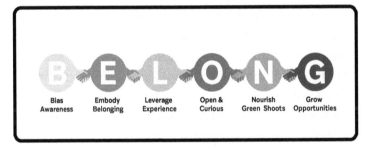

The BELONG model

The science behind the BELONG model

The BELONG model is based on my thirty years of business experience in leading people, managing teams, growing companies and helping global organisations to build more engaging and effective cultures, but don't take my word for it, look at the science.

Bias is known to impact discrimination. Mahzarin Banaji and Anthony Greenwald are perhaps the most influential proponents of implicit bias testing, also called the Implicit Association Test. Their work spans over twenty years and is summarised in *Blindspot: Hidden biases of good people*.[25] Their research shows that we use cognitive shortcuts to make decisions when facing a number of choices. When it comes to people, those implicit biases show up as discrimination, favouritism and judgements.

Authenticity as a term used to describe modern leaders has become almost common parlance these days, but its roots go back to the psychologists of the early twentieth century. In *The Undiscovered Self (Present and Future)*, Carl Jung talked about living a life of meaning, true to one's own values.[26] Maslow implicitly points to authenticity as our ultimate goal when he places self-actualisation at the top of his pyramid of needs.[27] Carl Rogers built on and expanded Maslow's view of self-actualisation by saying that every person could achieve their goals, wishes and desires in life if they were able to self-actualise, or grow into their most authentic self.[28] Brené Brown is a more up-to-date proponent of authenticity, which – based on her research of hundreds of executives – is one of the key qualities for making deeper connections. She equates authenticity with living wholeheartedly and puts this at the top of the ten guideposts for wholehearted living.[29]

The other cornerstone of the BELONG model is being open and curious. This is based on the practice of Appreciative Inquiry (AI) which was developed by Jacqueline Stavros, among others: 'At its heart, AI is about the search for the best in people, their organizations, and the strengths-filled, opportunity-rich world around them. AI is a fundamental shift... to "see" the wholeness of the human system and to "inquire" into that system's strengths, possibilities, and successes.'[30]

Isn't that exactly what we are trying to do in cultivating belonging? Seeing people for who they are and accepting them with all their strengths, possibilities and successes? Based on well-grounded and thoroughly researched traditional psychological models, the BELONG model offers a blueprint for creating a culture that is inclusive and where everyone feels like they belong.

Summary

In this chapter, we have looked at the BELONG model and its six important steps in learning to confidently create a culture that celebrates diversity and belonging. Each stage builds on the achievements of the last one. It is a model based on action, which is the only way we achieve change. By following the guidance in the successive chapters, and taking the actions suggested at the end of each, you will slowly build your toolkit as an inclusive leader and reap the benefits the changes will bring.

The person you are, the experiences you have had and the values you hold will be your passport into conversations and opportunities to build bridges with your under-represented employees. You may feel vulnerable putting so much of yourself out there on show for all the world to see, but we will do this in a gentle and thoughtful way. Your vulnerability is your strength and when you can come from a place of awareness, curiosity and compassion, you will find a greater depth of motivation and commitment not only in yourself but also in your employees.

In the following chapters, we will take each of the BELONG steps and go through what actions and new ways of working you can adopt to be a real champion of DE&I.

SUGGESTED EXERCISES

1. Think about what is motivating you to become a leader who actively supports and champions DE&I in your organisation.
2. Reach out to the Head of DE&I or HR in your organisation and find out what's happening and how you can help

5

Bias Awareness

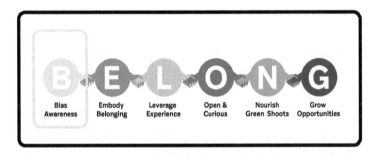

We all have bias. At the simplest end of the spectrum, it is about the preferences and choices we make. Do you prefer vanilla or chocolate chip? Are you right- or left-handed? Do you prefer to work out alone or in a class? At the more complex end, it is about the choices we make about who is in our life, what we believe and what we believe about others who don't hold the same beliefs. We cannot escape bias. It is often so deeply woven into the fabric of our culture, our upbringing and the family values we are taught, that it's hard to separate it from who we are. It takes effort to notice those biases and then choose to act from a place of neutrality.

Start where you are

As with everything, we need to start with exactly where we are. It is no use noticing the bias in others if you are not willing to do the work yourself. A lot of our bias begins in childhood. We are inculcated into a culture or belief system based on our parents' experiences, which leads us to see otherness in anyone who does not identify with the same points of reference.

I was brought up in an Irish Catholic household and went to a Catholic school and regular Sunday services. This was in the multicultural city of Birmingham, where our neighbours were from a range of cultural backgrounds, including white English and Church of England, Afro-Caribbean Christians, Indian Hindus, Pakistani Muslims. We all rubbed along OK and in my less aware days I would have said we had little bias, but that was not the case.

All of my parents' friends were from Ireland and Catholic. Their beliefs and values were shaped around the Catholic teachings, and they would show their displeasure at anything that was outside of their sphere with throwaway comments, looks or their tone of voice. Our neighbours were an Indian couple who were friendly and helpful. I was about eleven when they invited me to a wedding celebration in their house. Being a curious and open child, I was delighted and went. My mother, who was extremely anxious at the best of times, was not at all happy with this idea. Not that she disliked the couple, but that she felt they were not 'her' crowd and did not want her child in what she saw as a strange setting.

I attended the celebration and thoroughly enjoyed it. The colour, the smells, the talking (mostly they would speak in Hindu and then include me with a comment or a smile) and the food, which was exotic and spicy. This was still mid-1970s England and racial tensions were rife, so my neighbours' kind gesture to this insular and inward-looking white family was a great example of how bridges can be built across cultures and differences can be celebrated. If I had followed my mother's lead, I would have politely declined and missed out on a wonderful, diverse and colourful cultural experience.

I share this to illustrate that we often start where our parents are. Our childhood experience and our cultural references all have implicit bias within them and these can colour and shape our own. Some may serve us well, such as our cultural identity and our religious beliefs. Others may not, such as ideas of racial supremacy or privilege. An important step is to realise where your biases are and then pick out and address those that undermine your relationship with others, particularly people who have a different background and view of the world to you.

Bias, at its simplest, is preference and as individuals we all have preferences which differ from other people's. Preference helps us to shortcut our thinking and not dwell on simple decisions, and frees up important brain power to work out things that are new, novel or complex. By being aware of bias, we can see that not all bias is bad. In fact, it would be impossible to live in a world where we didn't already have a body of bias that shaped our thinking. Imagine if every decision we had to make – everything from what we wear to how we commute to work to what task we tackle when we get to the office – required all our attention and thought. Our brain would work at full capacity all the time and we would be exhausted.

Shortcuts are necessary to help us focus on what we need to and allow much of the rest to go on autopilot. This leaves room for fresh ideas and for us to learn and create new things. It is an extraordinary testament to the amazing human brain that has evolved to the complex machine it now is, far surpassing any other mammal on the planet. It is also our weakness.

If, like me, you were brought up in a monoculture household and socialised with others of the same cultural and religious beliefs, you were hardwiring a whole slew of shortcuts around what is normal based on this narrow point of reference. My parents did the same, their parents before them and so on. These hard circuits can be difficult to crack, but it starts with the first step that I took as a child, which was being curious. Why do people from other cultures see things differently to us? Why do they hold different beliefs? Why do they eat foods which differ from ours? Being curious about other racial, religious and cultural differences will help to bust some of your hardwired biases.

Know that it didn't begin (and doesn't end) with you

When I'm working with my coaching clients, I remind them that the challenges and themes that they are grappling with did not begin with them. Many of the traumas that we experienced in our childhood are to do with dynamics, decisions and disappointments that our parents faced, which were in turn handed down from their parents. It's the same when we think about barriers, inequalities and structures in modern society that have led to privilege for some and not for others. We like to believe that we are civilised and considerate and that we treat everyone as equal, but that is a myth that only those in a position of power and privilege can hold.

There is hardly a place in the world that has not been affected over its long history by invasion, war, conquest and cultural imprinting. History is defined by the victors, not those who were suppressed. Countless belief systems, cultures and ways of living that were inherent to different races have been eradicated over time. The victorious race systemically denies power to those it has suppressed, which includes denying them access to opportunities that may allow them to rise in the new order.

While we may have become more comfortable sharing power, and brought in laws to protect the more vulnerable members of our community, the inherent fabric of our society was born from inequality and remains unequal. The dominant culture (in my case white and Christian) remains dominant. Our political structures and media, our education, legal and policing systems all have a clear bias for white and Christian as the norm, and everything else as a deviation from that norm.

Biases can be changed with awareness, education and motivation. It might take years and decades for things to change at the structural level, but even in my lifetime, significant shifts have been made across these areas. We have not eradicated racism, sexism or homophobia, but these are no longer casually enacted without consequence in public life. All of us have biases which convey the superiority of our own cultural references over others.

The point is to realise that not only did it not start with you, but it also won't end with you. The first step to bias-busting is to be aware of it. In *White Fragility*, Robin DiAngelo encourages us to reflect on our subconscious bias by thinking back 'to the earliest time that your were aware that people from racial groups other than your own existed'. She wants you to question why those groups may or may not have lived in your area. If they lived in other areas, 'what images, sounds, and smells did you associate with these other neighborhoods?'.[31]

Educate yourself on the main issues

Culture and identities are complex. According to Infoplease, there are 'twelve classical religions – Baha'i, Buddhism, Christianity, Confucianism, Hinduism, Islam, Jainism, Judaism, Shinto, Sikhism, Taoism, and Zoroastrianism... five major races (Black, White, Asian, Indigenous American and Indigenous Australian) and over 190 countries'.[32] Just thinking of the kind of diversity that this represents is mind-boggling. With such diversity, ways of living and belief systems, how can we assume that any one of them is superior to the other? In our modern times, most of us would say we can't, yet we know that subtle biases exist in our societies.

Religious differences have caused much strife and warfare over the centuries. More recent warfare has been to do with economic disputes such as access to scarce resources like oil and gas. Dogma and ideology feature strongly in the post-World War II conflicts in places like North Korea, Vietnam, Iraq, Rwanda, Serbia and, more recently, Ukraine.

As we learn to coexist across borders and trade freely, we meet and experience different cultures and ways of doing things. Whenever you take on a new team, a new country or a new geographic region, you learn about their culture, beliefs and history, on which many of the modern-day norms will be built. When you are aware of and sympathetic to the cultural backdrop of the people you manage, you will be much more mindful of the best way to support, motivate and lead them.

Humans are complex beings and we comprise an array of identities that intersect, cross over and sometimes contradict each other. The iceberg model we discussed in Chapter 3 shows that there are probably more characteristics below the waterline – those unseen differences – than there are above it.

The identity iceberg reminds us to think of people and their identities in the round. We see the obvious differences above the surface, but there are many other unseen differences. You cannot know what is below the waterline for every person you manage, but you can show sensitivity to the possibility that these unseen differences exist.

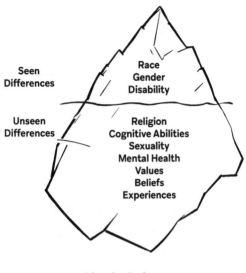

Seen
Differences

Race
Gender
Disability

Unseen
Differences

Religion
Cognitive Abilities
Sexuality
Mental Health
Values
Beliefs
Experiences

Identity iceberg

Intersectionality is when a person is affected by two or more different identity traits that would class them in a diverse category. I identify as a woman and as a lesbian, and this makes me more likely to experience some form of discrimination because of both traits. Another trait that could apply to me is socio-economic as I come from a working-class background in the UK; a further one would be ethnic, as I am the daughter of Irish immigrant parents. All these things make up my identity, and show how I differ from others in significant ways, particularly in the workplace.

I can remember certain points in my career where my intersectionality showed up in interesting ways. When I was the chief executive of a regional charity, I was surrounded by a group of amazing trustees. All of them except the founder were male, white and big-city businessmen. They came from a similar cultural mould, in that they were publicly schooled (which in the UK means privately educated), went to Oxford or Cambridge University (the top two red brick universities in the UK) and then entered the City of London and built their business career.

They were an incredibly supportive group of trustees for me as a young leader but every now and again our distinct differences would show through. I remember one occasion when we were visiting a school and it had Roman numerals over the door. One of my trustees said: 'Do you know your Roman numerals?' Beyond 1 to 10, I was lost. Another time we were hosting an event in a historical building and there was a Latin phrase over the door. 'How's your Latin?' I was asked. The answer was that it was non-existent. Both questions are perfectly normal for anyone who has been through a private education, but I went to an inner-city comprehensive school where education was not comprehensive at all, and Roman numerals and Latin were not on the curriculum. People like me were only expected to learn enough to get by in life and be ready for the world of work at sixteen. I was not offended by these questions and assumptions, but at the time I was left feeling lacking in some way when I could not answer them.

The identity iceberg reminds us of how complex every individual is. Our diverse backgrounds, experiences and identities offer uniqueness and difference. Rather than seeing the iceberg as a challenge, or even a minefield that you don't want to get caught out by, see it as an opportunity to explore the many ways your employees are defined. Whenever you are making decisions, creating a new product or service, promoting a team member or celebrating achievements, consider the iceberg diagram. You do not have to know all the unique identities that make up the people you manage, but coming from a place of awareness that we are all made up of multiple and sometimes competing identities allows you to move forward with sensitivity and compassion – the two essential ingredients for creating a culture of diversity and belonging.

Embark on a learning journey

When organisations embark on a journey to become more diverse and inclusive, leaders often feel overwhelmed and uncertain. This is natural when you must consider and manage things that have not been part of your experience to date or if you do not have a diverse trait or background that would inform your view. As mentioned in Chapter 3, the difficulty, if you have no lived experience of being in a minority or have not faced discrimination, is that you can feel overwhelmed.

I understand if your first reaction is that you are busy and you don't have time to go on a learning journey, but if you are reading this book, you are already well on your way. We are not talking of extensive study or even extensive reading, but more of opening your eyes to what exists around you and using a good dollop of humility to explore what you don't know.

One great example is from the current leader of BP group, Bernard Looney. I remember Bernard from when he was working in Trinidad, and he was always an approachable and humble leader. He believes in sharing his story, listening to others and taking clear action to bring about diversity and inclusion in the organisation of 60,000 employees that he now leads. He says: 'For me, it's very, very simple. People are treated with respect; people should absolutely feel safe – we shouldn't even have to question that. And, if ever we find people who are not supportive or aligned with that agenda, then they don't belong in our company.'[33]

You can take a leaf from Bernard's book as you start your learning journey, and a good place to start is knowing what you don't know. Where do you have direct experience of diversity and where are you lacking? If you have not been exposed to issues around gender, race, disability or sexual identity, then you need to find out what it means to have these identities. There is an extensive range of further reading at the back of this book, and there are many other places where you can find inspiration. Your employee group is a great resource, but caution is needed in how you proceed with this approach. You will not be thanked if you continually call out the only woman or person of colour in the room and ask them to supply opinions to represent that identity. A better way might be to find out if there are affinity groups (also called employee resource groups) where you can listen to participants' most pressing concerns and understand how you as a leader can help and address their needs.

Hayley Barnard, managing director and diversity strategist at MIX Diversity Developers, encourages people to take a few seconds to weigh up the consequences before responding in an unthinking (and perhaps biased) way. That alone is enough to break inbuilt or hidden bias. Another way to educate yourself would be to find some mentors from more junior levels in the organisation who identify with a diverse trait, and ask if you can meet regularly and share their perspectives and experiences. This is called reverse mentoring and can be instructive as you get to hear things that would otherwise not come out in your usual business forums. If this appeals to you, talk to HR first. Get terms of reference drawn up and ask them to help you find a suitable person. The last thing you want is unintended consequences which could have been avoided with a bit more planning and transparency.

Bias will show up at your work every day. It might be subtle and at a low level, but it will be there. It cannot help but be there since we all have some level of bias. Let's look at some of the main ways you can address this.

Gender bias

Gender bias shows up in many organisations, particularly if they have a technical or manufacturing base. Meetings and access to decision makers is often where it is most evident, and we see a bias towards the female majority if the organisation is healthcare or social care. As well as the more obvious way that gender inequality shows up in terms of seniority and pay levels, there are many subtle ways that it can manifest. To challenge this, ask yourself the following questions:

- In your meetings with your immediate reports, do you have an evenly balanced gender team? If not, think about why that is.

- Do you have an all-male or mostly male team, or is it the other way and you have all females?

- What might be the reason for the gender make-up of the team you have?

- What assumptions are there in your industry and in your organisation about who is best suited for a particular role, discipline or level of authority?

- When you think of a particular role, such as a technician, does your mind automatically conjure up a man?

A study by Zimmerman and West[34] published as far back as 1975 revealed how women get less airtime in meetings, are more likely to be interrupted and are less likely to be asked for their opinions compared to their male counterparts. According to gender communication expert Deborah Tannen,[35] men speak to determine and achieve power and status, but women talk to achieve connection. This was further evidenced by Fiona Sheridan, who concluded in her research that 'organisations may need to... facilitate the integration and assimilation of different types of talk, recognising that women and men use language differently.'[36]

If you have a mix of men and women in your meetings, observe who gets more airtime and who gets the least. Notice how much time people are speaking for and whether some people are being cut off in mid flow and others are dominating conversations. Another approach would be to record the meeting and then use a transcription tool such as Otter.ai to analyse contributions, airtime and interactions. If you see inequalities, then it is time to set some ground rules on how the meetings will be conducted going forward. Take time to present the evidence back to your team and ask them to help create a frame of reference that ensures that your meetings are fair and have a culture of belonging. You will be surprised how willing people will be to do this.

Racial bias

In Britain we have a 6.3% black, Asian or minority ethnic (BAME) population. In the USA it is much higher if we include Latinx populations, yet this racial and ethnic diversity is not reflected by those who hold the most power in our society. This can only be because some sort of bias is present. You can address this in your workplace by thinking about the following questions:

- When you look across your immediate team, their immediate team and the teams below them, what do you see as the racial diversity split?

- Does the racial diversity split in your organisation accurately reflect the population of your community?

- Do you find that for some jobs it is challenging to find a BAME candidate and, if so, what bias might exist in the discipline or occupational group to not attract more diverse candidates?

- When you are considering promotions, how much thought do you give to the importance of a racially diverse talent slate from which to decide?

Other ways that racial bias can show up is in social gatherings and celebrations. One organisation that I worked with used golf days as a reward for employees, but it favoured the partners over the junior employees. Most could not afford to go on such days and some came from cultures where golf was not a sport they recognised. In one focus group I was running, the Muslim office workers talked of the local pub being the only option offered for socialising with their colleagues. Of course, they could sit there with a soft drink and chat, but it was not a setting they would choose to go to and they did not feel they could relax and enjoy it.

A SAFE SPACE TO SHARE

In one manufacturing organisation, two leaders were making fun of some Chinese people in their team. They made funny voices and pulled their eyes wide to imitate the different facial features of someone from the Far East and then fell about laughing. A member of staff felt uncomfortable about this and told them and they just batted off her comment, saying it was harmless fun. She didn't take it any further, as she felt no one would take her seriously.

This employee's perception of the culture was that this sort of behaviour was tolerated and that HR would not act. This was based on what she saw as behaviour that was the norm for this organisation. The incident came out through focus group discussions. Without this voice or safe space, she said she would not have shared the incident. This is an example of a culture that tolerates and disregards discriminatory behaviour when it is viewed as low level or perhaps not serious enough to act on.

Other biases

Office banter can be another place where bias shows up. The subtle power plays that are enacted through humour or social sleights can be damaging to relationships. LGBTQ+ people are hyper-aware of how jokes about partners, relationships or public figures can reflect homophobia. If a group of men are talking about football and they think that one player is gay, they may make some joke about him playing for the other side, unaware that their colleague who is with them identifies as being gay, and leaving him in an awkward position about whether or not to speak up.

POCKETS OF HOMOPHOBIA

An employee who was part of the LGBTQ+ affinity group for their organisation – a global pharmaceutical company that was pretty advanced in its DE&I journey – wore a lanyard that clearly marked him out as a supporter of that community. He stepped into an elevator where he joined two male colleagues. During the elevator ride, one of the large men behind him said to the other, 'I think it's disgusting that we encourage homosexuality as a thing at work.'

Both men towered over this employee, who, with his LGBTQ+ lanyard clearly showing his allegiance, felt threatened being in such close quarters and hearing such hostile views which he did not believe it was safe to challenge. While he was able to go to other people for support after the fact, he did not feel the culture in his organisation had sufficiently evolved to tackle the issue head on. The DE&I initiatives had not brought everyone on the journey.

Neurodiversity is another unseen aspect of diversity which can show up in several ways. Perhaps the most well known and least understood is autism spectrum disorder (ASD) which often presents as brilliant technical skills and poor people skills. Other conditions include dyspraxia, which affects physical coordination, and dyslexia, which can make writing and particularly spelling a challenge. There are many other subtle conditions that make those who experience them different from neurotypical people. Are you aware of employees in your organisation who have one of these?

Awareness and understanding of these conditions, and small variations in work arrangements, can make a big difference to a person's sense of belonging. Someone with ASD will not like being in an open-plan office, as they find it difficult to filter out noises and distractions. If there is no alternative, then finding them a corner space and perhaps providing dividers will help create a calming work area. Someone with dyslexia might need additional software and specialised fonts to help them read and write in a way that's easier for them. If colleagues around them know and appreciate their needs, they are less likely to react negatively.

Social gatherings are great for morale and can help to bring people together, but this is another place where bias can show up. In *Inclusive Growth*,[37] author Toby Mildon describes a situation he was in. A wheelchair user, he worked in an office that was fully accessible and adapted to his needs, so no problem there. One Christmas, the celebration was held at a venue that was not wheelchair accessible. His protests were met with shrugged shoulders as if to say, 'What's the big deal?' His colleagues offered to carry him and his heavy wheelchair down to the venue if he wanted to go, ignorant to the lack of dignity he would suffer being beholden to others to get in or out and with no accessible toilet facilities.

Holding celebrations that are not sensitive to food choices can be off-putting to some employees. Has anyone checked whether the food is halal or kosher, if some would expect that? It may feel like it would be hard work to get the perfect balance to please everyone, but it comes down to intention and planning. If you want your events to be inclusive, consider everyone. If you want your culture to be one of belonging, factor in the diverse needs of everyone. If you are not sure, then simply ask.

Have a policy of zero tolerance

Zero tolerance as a term came from policing. In 1993, Mayor Rudolph Giuliani and NYPD Police Commissioner Bill Bratton introduced a style of zero-tolerance policing to New York City. They took the view that if there was tolerance for minor transgressions of the law, it was a slippery slope to ignoring larger infractions. This policy was unpopular with some but had a miraculous effect on the crime statistics of the city. While they significantly increased the burden on serving officers to act on situations they would previously have paid no attention to, Giuliani and Bratton reset the norms for the city. They signalled what was acceptable behaviour and what was not.

Zero tolerance has now entered common parlance as an approach to any policy infractions, particularly codes of misconduct in the business world. Having a zero-tolerance approach to discriminatory behaviour sends powerful signals across the organisation about what is expected of individuals and what behaviour will be tolerated or not.

What has been your tolerance to mild sexism, racism or homophobia in the past? Do you even recognise that such things have likely happened on your watch and you have not noticed? My guess is that if you are a leader of a large, complex and possibly global organisation, such things cannot have escaped you. What are you prepared to do about it now, as you raise your consciousness and notice your bias and that of others?

A good example of a zero-tolerance policy comes from when I was working as an interim director for a technology group. They were advanced in their DE&I practices and set a high bar to create a culture of belonging. A situation arose concerning a male leader who was seen as acting in a sexist manner in the way he held meetings, the social events that were organised and sometimes his slips of the tongue when alcohol had been consumed. He was an extrovert with a high-energy personality and was clearly more comfortable being one of the guys.

Several female colleagues made a complaint against what they saw as his unequal treatment towards them. Nothing out-and-out sexist, but enough to make them feel less valued than the men in the team. This organisation had a zero-tolerance approach to any behaviour that did not create a culture of belonging. Despite the strong protestations of his line manager and global director, after investigation this employee was dismissed. Afterwards, many female employees who had not put their voice to the initial complaint thanked me for the action and shared their own experiences at the hands of this ex-employee. None of this would have surfaced if we had not taken a zero-tolerance approach.

While you may not be able to directly influence your organisation's stance on a zero-tolerance policy, you can look at other ways to get your message across. Think of team meetings, town halls or social events: are there opportunities to address bias and send powerful messages around expected behaviours? A culture of inclusion and belonging can start with you and how you allow or don't allow the small sleights, jibes and micro-behaviours that belittle another group to pass. You will find you won't have to do it many times for people to get the message.

Summary

In this chapter, we have looked at how to become more aware of the everyday bias that you and others in your workplace may hold and how this plays out at work. We have acknowledged that we all have bias. Sometimes it's as simple as a preference for an ice-cream flavour and sometimes it's more harmful, like a bias to only hire white people. By being aware of bias, you can appreciate how it might play out in your own life and show up for others.

While biases are often nurtured through our early experiences with our family, school, religious groups and the wider community, they do not have to be life-long definitions of who we are and how we behave. The first step to breaking down bias is awareness; then comes understanding and for that to happen you need to educate yourself. Just as you worked to learn the skills of your trade, it is now incumbent on you to skill up to be a leader who champions diversity and inclusion. The age of social media has made this easier than ever and at the back of this book is a range of resources that will help you to become more aware of bias in and around your world and what you can do about it.

SUGGESTED EXERCISES

1. Take up the challenge of noticing the everyday bias at work.

2. Use the prompts in this chapter to reflect on how sexism or racism may be showing up at work.

3. Try this exercise to help you use your everyday lens to uncover and understand bias; it will only take about ten minutes of your time.

   - Start with simple things like your food choices, driving routes, the clothes you wear.

   - Notice the type of people you interact with and whether you have a certain 'type' of friend or colleague.

   - Look around in your organisation. What does the type of people that work there say about your brand? Is it a mainly 'white' brand? Is it mainly male?

   - Notice what you watch on TV. Do you see bias in the way that different racial groups are shown? Is there any diversity at all?

6
Embody The Values Of Belonging

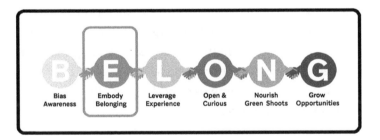

By observing and calling out bias in the workplace, we create a culture that feels safe and welcoming for everyone, regardless of their seen or unseen differences. To sustain this momentum of improving DE&I in your company, you need to dig deeper and connect your intention to your most important behavioural driver: your values.

I applaud inclusion as a concept and as a goal to achieve in the workplace, but it is not enough. It is often said that diversity is a fact and inclusion is a choice, meaning that it is how we treat people who are diverse that leads to inclusion. Many organisations on their DE&I journey focus solely on diversity. They set quotas, using a diverse slate approach, for recruitment of under-represented people, or targets on the number of female leaders, or they increase the number of people with disabilities. This is all great, but without the corresponding shift towards belonging, these diverse employees are faced with a workplace with a strong monoculture which is unsupportive and even hostile. They will not often stay in such a culture for long, meaning time, money and energy have been wasted attracting people to an organisation that was not ready to receive them. Inclusion means that teams are briefed about their new colleague. A sponsor or mentor from the senior ranks will support them and they have the listening ear and help of HR when they encounter resistance.

There is a higher goal that is worth aiming for which requires more work and more investment, but will bring greater rewards and greater sustainability, and that is belonging. Vernā Myers, a leading D&I expert, captures the essence of diversity and inclusion when she says: 'Diversity is being asked to the party, inclusion is being asked to dance.'[38] To that has been added a third element: 'Belonging is dancing as if no one is watching.'

Belonging goes beyond inclusion. It is not about seeing differences and welcoming them, or even not seeing differences and treating everyone the same; it is about celebrating individuality as a part of the collective whole. To go beyond inclusion and create a culture of belonging, you need to do the inner work necessary to change the outer façade of how you show up as a leader. This starts with understanding what drives you, which can always be found in your values.

Value-centred leadership

When we strip back all of our habits, priorities, beliefs and motivations, we get to our values. These are the things that make our life meaningful. Crucially, they will be different for everyone, even if we have come from the same life experiences, education or family group. Values are not something that can easily be elicited by observing someone's behaviour or finding out about their background.

If you had to name your top five values, would you know what they are? Most people find that a tough question to answer. It can be hard to articulate what is driving us if we have never had to reflect on it, yet those values are influencing us, whether or not we are aware of them. Values are the powerful coordinates of our own internal compass and will affect the way we live our life.

We are not generally encouraged to uncover our values, even though they are instrumental in all of our decisions and actions. Through my social work and master's degree in business administration, I have completed many self-assessments on my values and I find I am consistent about my top five. The benefit of knowing and owning our values is that we can explain our motivations and priorities in a much more coherent way. Everything comes back to our values and when we share them with others, they can respect where we are coming from and perhaps even relate.

Your organisation likely has a set of stated values which are highly visible and widely shared. Starting with these is a great way to unearth where your values sit. How closely do these values align with your own? Are there any that you feel uncomfortable sharing? Why? Knowing your top five values and comparing them with the values of your organisation will help you address questions such as:

- Does the organisation fit with my personal code and ethics?

- Are there ways I can show my alignment with organisational values?

- Do my own values provide a good basis for creating a culture of belonging?

Creating a culture of belonging is by nature a values-led exercise. We can only relate to others meaningfully if we understand why that is important to us. Your journey to championing DE&I in your workplace starts with this inner work. Setting out your agenda for diversity, equity, inclusion and belonging starts with defining why these qualities are important to you and how they relate to your own personal code. Your values are like compass points that help you to navigate the DE&I journey by making real and lasting connections with your employees.

While writing this book, I was part of a Book Builder© programme, where you spend as much time thinking about your own motivation and what you want to achieve in the book as what you are going to write. One of the exercises encourages you to take the core values test. I could have told you my number one value even before I did the test, but I might not have been able to say for certain what my top six were, as they may have shifted depending on the situation. As I honed my top six from a list of over 400, I recognised three things. First, that they had evolved over time. I did a similar test twenty years ago and my values were more outward-focused then. Second, that values affect all my work, yet I wouldn't use those words to describe it to people. Third, they confirmed the anchors of my life and how they colour my every decision and action, and that is comforting.

My top five values are:

- **Trust** – I believe humans are fundamentally good and work for everyone's higher purpose.

- **Love** – We are all made up of love. It is what binds us to each other and the world.

- **Joy** – When we are at our most connected, we feel joyful and guided by our inner light.

- **Courage** – Growth is our natural state and growth takes courage, which is bolstered by trust.

- **Spirituality** – The sense that there is a greater consciousness that supports the evolution of all life.

My core value, which sits above those five, is **Kindness**. There is a pithy phrase that I love: 'In a world where you can choose to be anything, choose to be kind.' Far from being soft or weak, kindness takes strength and belief. In fact, kindness needs values similar to my top five to be fully realised.

These values powerfully affected my motivation to write this book. They also show how my approach to DE&I is clearly linked to my values, and knowing these gives you a stronger mental image of me. Values convey who you are, what you do and why you do it. By uncovering your values, you will make sense of your own story and motivations and you will articulate them in such a way that people believe you, trust you and will want to follow you.

If you are curious about your top values, the full core values test is available at www.agents2change.com/theinclusionedge. Take the test and see what emerges for you.

Creating a culture of belonging

We have talked about how belonging is something more than inclusion. It goes further and builds more authentic and appreciative bonds with our employees through acceptance and acknowledgement of who they are. Many of the poor performance, high turn-over and dysfunctional behaviours in the workplace stem from a culture that is not sensitive to or listening to the needs of its people. Organisations that have a top-down approach to leading people imply a lack of trust towards their employees. Decisions and account-ability bubble up to the top, where power is tightly controlled. You may have worked in this kind of environment and even recognise this as your current organisation's culture or your own style of leadership.

To move away from a culture that is lacking in trust to one that is engaging and celebrates diversity, you need to start with your own behaviour. You may work with a leader whose style is not interactive or who is part of a senior leadership cohort which does not value empowerment, but you can still be a powerful influencer in shifting the culture in the right direction.

Some changes can be small. If you are used to opening meetings with your teams by delegating orders and setting expectations, change this to a listening ses-sion, asking for brief updates from around the table. This sends powerful messages of your willingness to hear from others. You could also look at revolving the role of chair and note-taker for meetings, to allow for quieter and newer team members to establish themselves. Showcasing the work of non-managerial staff is another great way to recognise their achievements and allow their talent to shine through.

How you recruit your people will also affect how well you create a culture of belonging. Over the last two decades, emphasis has been on meritocracy and cultural fit when hiring, with no awareness of how much bias was built into the talent processes. We are more likely to recruit and promote people like us and therefore squeeze out the opportunities for more diverse hires, but we are seeing the limitations of using these principles to build organisations. There are things you can do to reset expectations, such as insisting on more diverse candidates in your recruitment pipelines. You can also look at how recruiting is done. Are multiple interviews held without good reason? Is this putting off candidates who cannot take the time off work or afford the multiple journeys to your work location? Is the recruiting panel also diverse?

The onboarding process is rarely given sufficient consideration, yet it is often these early experiences that will determine if someone stays in the organisation. Take the time to reflect on your own approach. How well do you and your teams welcome new staff? What efforts are made to help people who are new to the industry, role or the geographic area? How well do you help them to feel like they belong?

If you don't know the answers to these questions, start digging until you find out more. Look at the onboarding process and see how it can have belonging as central to its design. It's often the little things that can make a difference. Some examples might be:

- The line manager doing a tour of the office with the new employee and introducing everyone

- Holding a team lunch on day one so the new member meets everyone (and has lunch bought for them)

- Making sure the new person has a desk to work at and ideally a little welcome sign on that desk

- Arranging meetings with everyone they need to know or who needs to know them to set them up well in the job

- Giving them a work buddy who can show them the ropes and help them out

None of these suggestions cost much in time or money, but they can make a huge difference in how someone feels about the job, the organisation and the team they will work in. This is true for all staff, but imagine if this is the first diverse employee in that team – maybe someone with an unseen diverse trait. Imagine how they will feel when this amount of thought is given to enable them to settle in and feel like they belong, showing a little kindness.

These are the building blocks you use to create a culture of belonging. It's not the broad sweeping statements of intent or the platitudes from the organisation's DE&I vision and strategy that make a difference, but the micro-behaviours and routines that are created within teams that encourage human connection and kindness. Teams with a culture of belonging don't see anyone as an odd man or woman out. Each person is respected for their contribution and their uniqueness. Differences are no longer a measure of how far from the norm an individual is, but to what extent they bring a new and interesting perspective. It is how you contribute that is valued, not how you fit in.

In a culture of belonging, collaboration and cooperation are highly valued. The team knows it is the sum of all its parts and ensures that each person is given everything they need to do their best work. A leader in such a culture is not about control, but about facilitating a process whereby people can shine. Your influence and ability to inspire others is directly linked to your values. Do your values support the idea of belonging as a way of working? How can your values help you create more freedom of expression for a sense of belonging to flourish?

The role of psychological safety

For a culture of belonging to be created, there needs to be a high level of support and trust. Remember the definition of belonging as dancing like no one is watching? What would it mean to have a workplace where people feel like they can do this? An environment where people feel able to express themselves and be fully heard and appreciated is at the heart of psychological safety, as William Kahn outlined in 1990: 'Psychological safety is being able to show and employ one's self without fear of negative consequences of self-image, status or career.'[39]

My school was not a psychologically safe place. When I left, I held the belief that I was not good at maths. The maths lessons were fraught with tension and fear. The teacher was an angry and intolerant man and at the first sign of kids being kids (talking or sniggering when his back was turned) he would swing round and throw the blackboard eraser – a hardwood block – with amazing accuracy at the offending child. We learned quickly not to make much noise and not to ask questions, as his withering response was almost as bad as being hit on the head by the eraser. This is the opposite of psychological safety and did a great deal to stunt my learning experience. It took almost a decade for me to build the confidence to return to the classroom and relearn maths, which it turned out I had an affinity with.

Even though such aggressive behaviour is not encouraged in the modern workplace, the absence of destructive behaviour does not automatically create a positive atmosphere. There has to be intent, action and signals from leaders that they are accepting of and encourage diversity and individual expression.

TOKENISTIC GESTURES

An example of not going quite far enough is a manufacturing company that was at the beginning of its DE&I journey. They had rolled out a comprehensive strategy, put in place solid policies and invested in celebrating key events.

One of those events was Pride, to show solidarity with the LGBTQ+ community. Some employees said that the whole process felt awkward. There was lots of communication; there were posters, badges, colourful lanyards, balloons and freebies left in communal areas, but if you were one of the many who chose not to be out at work, picking up any of the paraphernalia might signal your status. Without any ongoing support, many employees chose to ignore the items and avoid any conversations about the whole event. It didn't feel safe to do so.

Over the last decade, I've worked in many Internet-based companies. While the technology sector is generally ahead of the curve when it comes to belonging, they can still struggle to get it right. Leaders and teams are under such intense work pressure due to the fast-growing nature of these organisations, it's not surprising that unacceptable behaviours creep in. The biggest difference I have found in these organisations is that they will do what it takes to put it right. They build from the ground up and put people and their needs at the heart of that process. They also consider the architecture of their physical workplaces. Much of the area is given over to meeting, chilling and play spaces. This turns traditional thinking about work on its head. It says that we know you are a hard worker, but you need time to relax, even while you are at work. Far from creating an army of layabouts, this kind of workplace motivates employees to work harder, because they know they are cared for.

Employees in these environments often work longer hours than traditional organisations and although they have fun and access to food and even free alcohol after work, these are not the focus of their attention. They come to work because they feel cared about, looked after and supported. They work hard because they believe in the organisation and what it is striving to achieve and they stay because they have a leader that supports and encourages them and helps them to grow in their role.

If I had to define one thing that separates these newer technology industries from more traditional ones, it would be accessibility, which starts with thinking through the physical space. Every one of the technology organisations has accessible buildings, and they address several needs at once, which is belonging in action. They allow for wheelchair access throughout, and not just through the front door; they often have

Braille alongside text signs; they have lighting that is sensitive to a whole range of conditions, including dyspraxia and epilepsy. While most workspaces are open plan, there are plenty of small rooms and alcoves that help people with conditions like ADHD to cope with noisy environments. Thought is given to the colour schemes, which optimise mood and energy without being overstimulating. This level of person-centred design speaks volumes about a commitment to belonging.

In Chapter 3 we mentioned fireside chats, where there is clever psychology at play. Spaces are often created in an amphitheatre design to bring employees together to hear from leaders or guests. The leader is at the bottom, in the arena, so to speak, while the employees are in ever-increasing rows towering above them. This lessens the impact of power distance between employee and leader and leads to great engagement.

Your organisation's physical space may not have the same functionality, but you could cultivate the idea of formats and conversations which are informal, allow for two-way dialogue and are about human connection. In the next chapter, we will cover what you can leverage from your own experience to build these bonds.

Summary

This chapter has been about the building blocks you need for your people to feel accepted, welcomed and understood in your organisation and teams. Striving to create the conditions that signal acceptance and belonging to your employees takes effort but brings big rewards. It starts with you and how you identify and articulate your own values, what your intentions are and how you convey these.

Inclusion, which is about bringing people into the fold and helping them to settle in, is a great start but we need to be more ambitious. We need to signal that it is not fitting in that is valued, but contributing to great performance in whatever way feels right to the employee. Belonging is about making space for people to express themselves fully, as opposed to just making sure they have a place at the table.

The other building block is harnessing psychological safety. At its heart, this is about how safe your people feel in sharing parts of their innermost identity at work; for example, cultural background, ethnic identity or sexual orientation. The more the tone of psychological safety can be created, the more the culture of belonging will develop.

SUGGESTED EXERCISES

1. Take the core values test at the back of this book to identify your top six values and the core essential value that drives you.

2. Then review your organisation's values. Reflect on each one and how much your own values identify with or differ from them. Consider how you can tie your own values more closely with your organisation's values in how you describe your motivations and priorities to your employees.

7
Leverage Experience

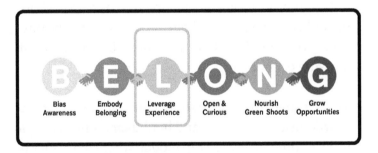

As we build foundations for an inclusive environment that celebrates diversity and belonging, we need to do the inner work, to find the nuggets of gold in our own experience that will pave the way for others. You might feel that you have nothing to share, but in this chapter we will look at how experiences have challenged you and shaped who you are. Even if they were not purely about being in a minority or being excluded, they will serve a purpose in showing your humanity authentically and building bridges to your employees' experiences.

Self-disclosure as a route to authenticity

Brené Brown talks about authenticity as the willingness to be vulnerable. Her research found that those who had the courage to be vulnerable in front of others were more resilient and garnered more respect. Far from being weaker by acknowledging their vulnerability, they appeared stronger, because they understood and knew their weaknesses, but did not let them define them. Brown asserts: 'Vulnerability is not winning or losing; it's having the courage to show up and be seen when we have no control over the outcome. Vulnerability is not weakness; it's our greatest measure of courage.'[40]

Many leaders struggle to show vulnerability. They use power distance to create and hold their authority. This is the traditional leadership model, where the leader is remote, inaccessible, formal and authoritarian in style. This kind of leader does not signal or model a culture of belonging, nor do they enable psychological safety, since their real self is hidden from the people they lead. If you recognise this more traditional leadership style, the idea of opening up and talking about yourself might leave you in a cold sweat. Let me reassure you this is not an all-or-nothing disclosure scenario.

It is about knowing who you are and what is important to you. Sharing your journey, the highs and lows and the underlying motivations that helped you to get over setbacks along the way, is deeply motivating for your employees. Your story helps them to consider their own. Would they see their career in the same way? Would they have the same resilience as you found when dealing with challenges? Your employees know you through your stories and your stories reveal who you are.

When I'm encouraging my clients to come up with stories which describe who they are, I suggest they go to key points in their timeline – transitions when a big change was inevitable. How they dealt with those transitions and what they learned from them is where the magic can be found. Think of some of your big transitions and how you handled them. For example:

- Your first day (or year) at school

- Your first day at secondary/high school

- Your first month at university

- The first day of your first job

- Meeting the love of your life (if appropriate)

- The birth of your child/children (if appropriate)

- The first day in this organisation

- The first day of this job

These will provide examples of when you have been out of your comfort zone. Write down your experiences for each of these events. Think about it in terms of the following questions:

1. What was I feeling before this event?

2. How did I feel during the event?

3. How did I feel afterwards?

4. How were my thinking and perception altered as a result of this experience?

These four prompts are at the heart of storytelling. All stories start with a person facing an event through which they learn something about themselves or their environment.

By writing these experiences down, you will trigger memories and emotions that may have been deeply buried and cause you discomfort. My advice is to sit with it for a while and see what comes up and why. Not only will this help you process long-forgotten challenges, it will lead to invaluable insights into the traumas, difficulties and insecurities your employees might have felt when they joined your organisation and teams. These insights help you share your vulnerability meaningfully. While it may feel counterintuitive to everything that you have read and understood about leadership, the more you can authentically share aspects of your vulnerability, the truer and stronger you will come across as a leader.

Everyone has an exclusion story

I encourage you to collect stories that describe times of struggle and difficulty in your life. These will be examples of when you have felt lonely, unsupported, unappreciated or excluded and can illustrate an understanding of the many challenges your employees might face. They may well be an allegory of not one, but many stories from your life that illustrate some aspect of your own vulnerability, but also how you found strength from that experience.

When you have gathered, recited and practised delivering two or three exclusion stories of your own, you can use these judiciously for discussions with big or small groups within your organisation and when you are addressing external groups. You will find it becomes easier each time you share and things you thought you would never say aloud start to come naturally to you. You will also see the magic that happens with this kind of personal disclosure. People will thank you; they will share their stories and they will feel inspired. You will have conversations that you have never had before in the workplace, around human potential, overcoming obstacles and living with challenges. In short, you will understand your people far more, because you have taken the time to understand yourself and share what you found meaningfully.

Digging for your own exclusion stories starts with the list we mentioned earlier around some firsts or challenges in your life. They could include experiences with a family member, such as a parent, a partner or a child. They could involve working or travelling to another country or when you had a physical challenge of some sort. We have all experienced exclusion at some point, a time when we felt like we were not welcome, that we did not belong or that we were the only one with this issue. I have many exclusion stories I can share. They have different themes and tones, depending on what aspect of myself I think it is helpful to be open about. I will share one with you now about ethnic diversity.

When I was eight years old, I was out with my mother one day and I noticed that she was unusually tense. My mother was always a nervous sort, but I knew this had a different feel to it. Shopping or on the bus, I could feel her hand tightly gripping mine and the set of her mouth and face seemed grim.

My mother was a chatty woman, but on this day she was unusually quiet, leaving shops without saying a word and only nodding to the bus driver. We entered the hairdresser, which my mother would have visited regularly. As we went into the salon, all the noisy chatter stopped and I could feel the hostility. I remember being confused and looking up to my mother, wondering what was going on. My mother's grip on my hand grew tighter and she stayed quiet.

This was at the time of the IRA pub bombings in Birmingham that killed twenty-one people and injured almost 200 more. There was a strong anti-Irish sentiment that swept through the country and was particularly strong in Birmingham. Even at that young age, I sensed the otherness that my mother felt. I sensed she did not feel she belonged in that city or that neighbourhood and by association neither did I.

When you consider your exclusion stories, think about the many times in your life when you or a loved one has been challenged. Write those stories and share them with someone close. Ask what they felt was more important or less important in the story and what they felt it told them about you. Practise a few and build up your library. Then, as you address your teams through different forums like fireside chats or small group meetings and you want to convey your understanding of exclusion, you can start with one of these stories.

The power of storytelling

We are hardwired for stories. Our history as modern humans stretches back tens of thousands of years, yet our written word is only about 5,000 years old. Historically, how we learned about our world, the norms of our tribe and the expectations of us as individuals was through the fireside stories that were passed down orally from generation to generation.

Stories are powerful. Our brain listens and memorises stories far better than a written report of the same length. We have neural connectors and memory storage specific to learning and retelling stories, so a story will have a much greater impact on a group than a policy, a platitude or a command.

When we share stories of exclusion, we are putting everyone in a more relaxed state. Have you ever noticed how children immediately relax when they know it is story time? As adults we do something similar. Our curious mind takes over and we stay quiet and see where the story leads us. This has a much stronger engagement hook than any other communication tool at our disposal.

Each story has an arc to it. This is akin to the hero's journey, where an unsuspecting character has lived a blithely quiet life, wishing for adventure. They set out to see the big city, or the world, or to slay the dragon. They hold beliefs that the world is constructed according to their own experiences. The quest and the journey are then about how the protagonist must either change their beliefs about the world or who they are in relation to it. Through inner shift comes outer shift in the form of achieving their quest.

Stories are about learning about the world and our beliefs. They explain how we grow and learn through narrative. They help us make sense of our inner and outer world. They enable us to reflect on who we are, where we are and what we want to achieve. They are also the way we bind people to a cause, a tribe or an organisation. You can create a culture of belonging by honing and practising your storytelling skills and by encouraging others to do the same. Your exclusion stories signal your awareness of exclusion in a powerful and meaningful way.

An example that proved effective for opening the conversation and helping the organisation move forward is from the CEO of a global food group. When he launched the DE&I programme in his organisation, he started with his own story.

JACK'S STORY

Jack hosted an event for all his employees to launch DE&I in his area. He was open about his lack of exposure to many cultures and, therefore, his limitations: he came from a country with little racial or cultural diversity and his family and immediate reports all came from the same culture.

Jack explained that he had been brought up in rural Southeast Ireland to Irish parents, who themselves were from Irish parents. He went to an Irish Catholic School, played Irish sports growing up and went to university in Ireland. 'There was not much diversity where I was from,' he explained. 'That does not mean I don't appreciate it now. I want your help to learn. I want you to know that I support all the different cultures that are part of my organisation. So, if you feel there is something I have not understood, or that I have acted in ignorance, then please tell me. We all must learn and that includes me.'

The effect of this honest and humble approach to launching DE&I was astounding. It was a watershed moment for the business and the comments of appreciation came flooding in.

Jack learned that his lack of exposure to diversity was not the issue, but only his attitude to it. By admitting his limitations and asking for help from his employees, he created a groundswell of support. He made himself vulnerable, not by sharing major traumatic events in his life, but by acknowledging his limitations and his willingness to learn from others. What was unusual about Jack's approach was that he didn't speak as a CEO but as the person behind the role. This made it a powerful moment for the organisation and is part of the reason why their efforts to build a culture of belonging have continued to be so successful since. He set the right tone by acknowledging that, at the heart of belonging, is the universal human experience. It is not how far you have travelled, or how many people you have met that matter, but your willingness to acknowledge and learn from others.

Your storytelling will help to convey your willingness to learn from others as you will share times when that is exactly what you did. You will also help your teams and employees share their stories in a way that honours and respects their journey and their backgrounds.

This is how we build a culture of belonging – one story at a time.

Learning from the greats

Some companies that are great at belonging are headed up by inspirational leaders who are themselves open, authentic and humble. They build a culture that is open, supportive and welcoming to people from all walks of life. We can learn a lot from how these leaders make themselves available and human, yet still maintain their authority as a leader.

Richard Branson is perhaps one of the most widely recognised entrepreneurs in the world, with a brand that has expanded across many sectors, services and products. Virgin is a brand experience which sets high expectations in the minds of its consumer. People associate Virgin with being fun, energetic, customer-focused and of excellent quality. Whether it is banking or air travel, people choose Virgin over other brands because they trust it to look after them and think about their needs as an individual. Richard Branson has done a lot to create that brand experience, not only through his own values but also through his style of leadership.

Branson is informal and accessible. He created the idea of fireside chats before they were even a thing in the Internet-based sector. He understands implicitly that if people are to follow him, they need to have a sense of who he is and how he sees the world. Richard interacts regularly with his staff, arranges weekly or monthly 'ask me anything' sessions and meets new recruits during their onboarding process. He is casually dressed, sits in a relaxed posture and makes jokes. He always answers as honestly as he can and asks questions back to his employees. People love working for him, as his humility, honesty and directness show them who he is. They know he cares for them and that he wants them to enjoy their experience working for him or one of his companies, which is why he has engagement and retention levels way above any of his competitors.

Another leader who has a similarly open style is Brian Chesky of Airbnb. From a simple idea of helping conference attendees by offering a bed for a night when all the hotels were full, a global accommodation platform was born. Belonging is important to Brian. Airbnb was built on kindness and hospitality. 'Be a host' is one of their core values. As well as being an exceptional work environment that embraces diversity and belonging, Airbnb has a caring and accessible leader. Every week there is a CEO Q & A that is aired around the world, and employees in San Francisco can meet with Brian and ask him anything, which they do. He believes in being accessible and transparent, sharing his issues, concerns, dreams and hopes. Airbnb employees will go a lot further than the extra mile to deliver for him, because they believe in what he has created and how much he cares for each of them as individuals.

It might not be the right style for you to rock up at work in jeans or chinos, fist-bump every employee and relax into a sofa to chat to whoever is around. Perhaps all that is required from you is a little softening of the power distance that typifies your role or style. This could be small gestures like holding informal lunches for teams, or even meeting with new employees and asking what attracted them to the company. Rather than waiting for the larger and more formal town-hall events, perhaps you could hold smaller regional events, or visit teams in more remote locations. By being more accessible, you will hear things that would not otherwise arise and you will gain invaluable insights about yourself and your employees that can help to bridge gaps, ease tensions and build a better, more connected culture of belonging.

Summary

In this chapter, we are digging for the gold – your own experiences. You can find inspiration for your own stories from many aspects of your life. Sharing these will build meaningful bridges with your employees' experiences of exclusion, and will give you an awareness of the struggles of others. We often inure ourselves to our own suffering and, as a result, do not see suffering in others. Becoming sensitive to times of hardship in your life will open doors to appreciating it in others.

SUGGESTED EXERCISES

1. Uncover three stories from your life and write them down. Practise telling them, initially alone and then with someone you trust to give honest feedback. What did they get from the story? How did they see you at the beginning of the story and did this change at the end? What did they want to hear more of? Less of?

2. Consider ways you can introduce more relaxed meetings and conversations into your employee events.

8

Open And Curious

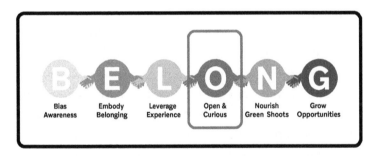

This step in the BELONG model is all about show-ing an interest in your employees and getting to know their stories and experiences. This is where you learn about their hopes and dreams and what makes them tick. You might question why you need to know all this. For some people, it will be enough to keep things at a professional level with little personal dis-closure, but that is not often the case for the majority.

What we crave above anything else – money, success, a big job title – is human connection. Feeling heard, understood and respected is a universal human need.

Remember Brian Chesky's core value for Airbnb: 'Be a host'? What he meant by that is that if you invite a stranger into your home, you will make them welcome. You will make sure the room is ready for them, that you have food they can enjoy, that your home is warm and welcoming. You are likely to sit down and chat with them for a while, find out a bit about them. You might enquire what brought them to you and what are they looking to do while with you. If you are a good host, you will do your utmost to make them feel welcome.

Imagine if all organisations treated their new employees this way. The turnover rate would plummet, because people would immediately feel like they were in the right place. If you reflect on the onboarding experience of your employees, how many behaviours of belonging are baked into that process? Even if your organisation has not put a lot of effort into onboarding employees, you can model what a welcoming organisation feels like. You can help create a culture of belonging. In this chapter we'll explore how having an open and curious mind can help you uncover the stories of others. What challenges have they overcome and why are they here, now, working with you?

In *The 7 Habits of Highly Effective People*, Stephen Covey encourages readers to 'Seek first to understand.'[41]

Because we are on transmit mode in so many of our daily interactions, we often forget to check if we have understood the needs of the other person. This is especially true if your time is in constant demand. Like most busy people, you will have shortcuts to get work done, clarify expectations and delegate tasks.

We have seen how our personal stories have the power to build bridges and open up valuable conversations with employees. Before you share these stories, you will need to be good at listening to your employees and hearing their stories, their needs, their concerns. If your thoughts are immediately defaulting to 'I don't have time for this' then catch that idea before it takes hold and change it to 'I need to do this. This is important.' Much of your busyness will be generated by your thinking. If you are feeling harried and overwhelmed, that is probably the sign of a busy mind. In case you didn't know this, let me share a secret. A quiet mind will get more done than a busy mind. Start with your thoughts; change the inner narrative to change the outer experience.

A mindset that appreciates the unique aspects of everyone's story is central to the concept of belonging. You take an active interest in each of your employees so that you see the whole person, not just the job title or the role they fulfil. You know about their kids, you know what college they went to, or that they have an elderly mother a few hundred miles away who they worry about. You know that they have a passion for numbers, and that they could do much better if you moved them into the accounts department. You appreciate and understand their stories and through these you learn who they are.

Open enquiry

Open enquiry is a technique that allows you to be in the moment with a person and give them your entire attention without judgement or agenda. You engage in conversation through open questions that explore how the other person sees the world, without imposing your own view. The point of open enquiry is to have as little of your own presence dominating the situation as possible, so that you can see, hear and understand the other person.

In open enquiry, you use open questions such as 'How?', 'Why?' and 'When?' These are exploratory questions and will often yield interesting and extensive answers. Every follow-up question would be similarly open-ended, to allow the enquiry to continue and go deeper. In addition to the type of questions used, it is important to think about your body language, tone of voice and eye contact.

Body language

We rarely consider how much our body language conveys about our state of being and how quickly it is picked up on by others. Even minor adjustments in how we hold ourselves send powerful signals to others. We are exceptional at picking up on nuances in body language, even if our thinking brain isn't always good at interpreting them. This is because the majority of our human experience has been nonverbal. It is thought that the language we rely on nowadays began to develop around 50,000 years ago, yet our evolutionary journey started about a million years before that.[42] Much of our human development relied on nonverbal skills and instincts which are so deeply ingrained they barely scratch the surface of our conscious mind. Body language was the first way that early humans learned how to determine friend from foe.

If you want other people to relax and open up in your company, you need to adopt body language that conveys that you are a friend. This will have a much greater effect than telling someone to relax. The best way to do this is by connecting with your body, checking in with it by bringing awareness to your breath and seeing if it is tense anywhere. If you notice tenseness, ask your body to relax. A simple check in to each main area (face, shoulders, arms, legs etc) and a silent mental note to relax is often enough for you to come across as warm and welcoming. Your breath is another powerful tool for relaxation. Often our breath is shallow and only held in the upper chest area. Deepening your breath to your lower belly area by using circular breathing (in through the nose and out through the mouth) will have a significant impact on relaxing your body and mind.

Another big part of our body language is our facial expressions. Relaxing our body is important, but by softening the area around our eyes and mouth we send powerful signals that we are receptive to the other person. The easiest way to do this is to smile. If you have a meeting with your staff where you want them to open up and tell you some home truths, making sure you are relaxed and open in your own body language will help enormously.

Voice

The other area to be aware of is your tone of voice. If you are using open questions and a relaxed body language, but are still speaking in a sharp, clipped tone, you may struggle to engage and hear your people. Tone of voice is one of the nonverbal cues we use to pick up on the emotional state of another person. We can tell immediately if someone is strained, angry or stressed by the quality of their vocal tones.

When you want to create a relaxing and inviting conversation, use a gentle and quiet tone. You need to drop an octave or two below conversational and slow your speech to help create the right ambiance for open enquiry, which signals that you have the time and the interest to listen to others.

Eye contact

We have to take the Goldilocks approach to eye contact. Not too little, not too much, but just enough for it to feel comfortable and attentive. If we have pressurised jobs and are swamped with demands, we can delude ourselves by thinking we are multitasking when we respond to someone without bothering to make eye contact. We are writing an urgent report when one of our supervisors comes in and asks a question. We give them the answer, they go away and we continue with the report. It's OK that we have not looked up or at the person because all they needed was the answer. Right? Wrong! Multitasking allows you to do many things badly at the same time. You probably constructed a poor sentence in your report and left your supervisor a bit miffed as she needed more information, but you seemed in no mood to talk.

If you recognise this harried, overworked leader as yourself, you have probably got in the habit of only giving people cursory eye contact, as you find yourself distracted by the next task on your list. It's time to do some work to get that right and improve your levels of engagement. If you are not one for eye contact, then it will feel strange and perhaps uncomfortable. A trick to help is to look at someone at the bridge of their nose. This can lessen the feeling of intimacy or threat that can sometimes be engendered with eye contact, and the other person will feel seen and, by virtue of that, heard. When we don't have eye contact during a conversation, we find it hard to remember what was said and if we were asking for something, we will go away feeling that our needs were not met. Taking time to increase your eye contact will greatly enhance the communication with your direct reports and wider team.

Practising open enquiry

If some of these skills are new or rusty, the best place to practise is at home with a loved one or close friend. Perhaps start a conversation about what the person wants for a birthday gift, where to go for dinner or the next holiday destination – a conversation that requires you to know more about their needs and wants than your own. Using the three key aspects of open enquiry – open questions, relaxed body language and good eye contact – ask between five and seven questions before you offer anything of your own opinion or view. Each time you receive an answer, follow up with another question that delves deeper into their preferences. When you have fully exhausted what they want, why they want it and when they would like it to happen, check out if there are any more questions you need to ask.

Throughout this process, you do not offer your opinion or view. Even if you disagree with what you hear, you keep listening, relaxing, nodding and gently encouraging the person to open up and share their perspective of the world. At the end, share what you heard, literally play it back. If this is something you have not done in your conversations with a partner or friend for a long time, expect it to yield some surprising and beneficial results. Magic happens when you take the time to listen and hear someone else, because we do it so little in life. Once you have seen the benefits it can yield in your personal life, you are ready to use it in the work setting, which will also bring some unexpected positive surprises.

The first uncomfortable conversation

Once you have crossed the metaphorical Rubicon and opened up conversations that use open enquiry, you will start to see the value these conversations bring in the workplace. This can feel challenging if it is a big departure from the way you usually do business and your usual conversations. It will require some thought and preparation and you may need some HR support or a professional coach to help you work out how to integrate this new way of communicating into your work life authentically.

Open enquiry works best by departing from tried-and-tested meetings and going for something more informal, like a fireside chat or an open mic idea. This already signals to employees that the meeting will differ from the norm and will pique their interest. You might start small, such as a team meeting with your immediate reports where you open up with questions that you rarely take the time to ask, such as: 'How are you doing? Tell me what things are like from your perspective – I'd like to hear that.'

Allow yourself to relax into a process of listening to your team and their concerns and issues. Notice your inner resistance in the form of negative mental chatter or being anxious to push forward to the 'real' agenda, as this will also tell you something about your reluctance to have genuine conversations that connect on a more human level.

When we hide behind the busyness of work, we tend not to see people, but a mound of tasks. You may even notice some resistance as you read this, and find yourself thinking, 'Well, what's wrong with that?' On one level, there is nothing wrong with it. On another level, it erodes any human connection and moves us further from our goal of creating a culture of belonging. My simple way of opening conversations is by doing a round robin of, 'How are you doing? What's on your mind?' I open many of my meetings this way and have found it helps with team cohesion and brings matters to my attention that may have taken a lot longer if we had stuck to the formal agenda.

An example of the benefits of this approach is when I was bringing together a team of HR professionals who were situated in different continents. After a few guided mindful breaths, the first thing we did was to get to know each other, and the understanding and appreciation that came out of that sharing helped the team to gel. One particular story that still stays with me and helped to bring a sense of belonging to the newest recruit was when she shared childhood experiences that encouraged us to put our 'first world' troubles into perspective. Was it relevant or necessary for the meeting? No. Was it essential for team cohesion and building belonging? Yes. Here is what she told us.

A HOUSE IN KASHMIR

I was born in the Kashmir Valley, in a house where several generations lived together. My grandfather was a civil servant. One of his big dreams was to build a house that was big enough for all of us to live in and he finally achieved that after years of scraping together funds and building it one stone at a time.

I remember how exciting it was to move into the house. We all ran around looking at the rooms and finding the special ones assigned to us children, much bigger than what we had before. I was perhaps six years old.

Then trouble erupted and my grandfather was shot and badly wounded. His life was threatened and he was told if he did not go, he and all his family would die. We fled to India and had to live with relatives.

For two years, I slept on a balcony as there was not enough room for all of us. Although my grandfather survived being shot, something died inside of him and he never recovered after we left Kashmir. I have never been back. My parents tell me it is very beautiful but I have too much trauma associated with it to return.

What we were told in that share bore no resemblance to the HR priorities or the business agenda that we had all flown to Singapore to discuss. It had everything to do with making our new recruit feel welcomed and that she belonged. This was her first day with us and she felt able to talk about a painful and traumatic memory. There was not a dry eye in the room, but we all let her know how much we appreciated her sharing that with us and that she was now part of a supportive team that she could count on. I am not expecting your meetings to unearth deep revelations, but there may be little snippets of information which tell you how your people are feeling, what is troubling them or what they are focusing on. From this you will get a good idea of how they are doing and what support they need.

Another approach is personal disclosure. This needs to be part of an agreed agenda prepared in advance. I have seen team events and awaydays work well when sessions in inclusion and belonging involve hearing from people who have experienced exclusion and are happy to share how it transpired and what they did to address it. In one organisation, the director put in a ninety-minute session on belonging as part of a two-day team building event. He used storytelling to great effect. Not just his own story, but one of his immediate reports shared hers as well. They took about ten minutes each to describe what they experienced and what happened, but those twenty minutes were transformational. Both helped with the facilitated discussions about belonging that followed and identified several actions that would help to create more belonging for their teams.

REDUCED TO NOTE-TAKER

Sharon shared her experience working in a financial company in the USA. She was a young, ambitious woman working in an all-male team. She would constantly find herself delegated to note-taking or making coffee. Her boss would refer to her as 'doll' or 'honey' which felt very uncomfortable.

It was hard to find her feet in this role, as she was treated as the secretary, even though she was a fully qualified accountant. Then the line manager made subtle sexual innuendos that progressed to him making passes at her. The lingering hand on the shoulder, the staring at her breasts while talking, the brush against her bottom as he passed. She complained to HR, but found they were reluctant to do anything.

Sharon decided that the only thing she could do was leave, but it made her much more assertive to stand up for her rights and not be belittled or objectified again. Now she loves her job and feels respected and valued.

In this event, there was no big PowerPoint deck about belonging. There was no theory or model of best practice, just stories and perspectives that enabled the forty people in the room to hear the issues and understand what belonging is and what it is not in a unique, non-threatening way. This led to facilitated discussions in small teams sharing personal stories of when employees had felt they belonged and when they did not. They came up with ways the team could create more of a sense of belonging in how they worked – a simple and powerful format to bring the concept of belonging to life.

This example is illustrative of what can be done with a little imagination, thought and courage. Think about how to bring a conversation to your teams. Think small, perhaps starting with your immediate reports and having a session where issues can be shared, heard and understood. It might even be appropriate to share one of your own exclusion stories here, but if you do this, perhaps ask one of your close colleagues to share something from their life and experiences as well. It's essential to work out the details in advance, as the last thing you want to do is put someone on the spot and make them feel uncomfortable. A well planned session will bring more candour, support and curiosity, which will all lead to better performance.

Receiving challenging feedback gracefully

One thing you will have to be ready for as you open up conversations about diversity, inclusion and belonging is the heated reactions and powerful emotions that will arise. Do not expect everyone to be on the same page, or even the same chapter around these issues. There will be many challenging and diverse views, some of which may make for difficult hearing. Accept that DE&I is emotive and will cause people to express views that differ from your own. Change comes through seeing things differently and then acting accordingly, and in terms of DE&I that means having the controversial debates necessary to help people who have held the power over minority groups or acted in insensitive or insulting ways. We cannot move forward without understanding. This is crucial to creating a culture of belonging and, although it can be a deeply uncomfortable experience, it will reap great rewards in the long term.

To hear and appreciate another person's anger or anguish, you need to be humble. You need to understand the root cause. Our society is not equal. We have barriers and rules that keep certain people out at the expense of others being in. While it is getting better, we still have a long way to go to see true equality. You may never have experienced the setbacks caused by one of your characteristics, or a lifestyle choice, but many of your people will. Nothing makes people angrier than injustice. When you open up these conversations and face the frustration and anger your people feel about injustices in the world, your most important task is to listen with curiosity and humility and begin to understand their issues. Most people who share their frustrations do not want you to do anything. You may want to go into problem-solving mode, because doing something makes strong emotions easier to deal with. This is a form of resistance and it does not help in the long run. Most people who are giving you the benefit of their experience are not attacking you. They are in fact showing you this is a safe place for them to express who they are.

Let me share an experience I had where some strong emotions were aired. At a large leadership seminar in the USA, I was asked to lead the DE&I part of the proceedings. This was a strong, vocal and collaborative group of about 120 leaders. I made the mistake of first giving a presentation about aspects of diversity in terms of human behaviour. Starting by transmitting, rather than listening, cut me off from the feelings of the group. Unbeknown to me, the previous speaker, one of the company directors, had made an off-the-cuff remark which sparked a lot of frustration. My session tipped that over into downright anger. Two people were vocal, one a white lesbian and the other a black woman. They both had different issues but felt that they experienced patronising behaviour from their senior leaders and wanted them to 'get with the program'.

I know that the leaders of the event felt uncomfortable about this outpouring, but I saw it as positive. What these two women were saying, along with many others who joined in the debate, was that this was not enough. My olive branch of a presentation was not enough. The previous speaker talking about 'diverse folks' was not enough and the leaders of these teams, sitting passively, was not enough. I understood and I agreed. I have done things differently since, but I also see that it was a watershed moment. The debate that occurred while people were feeling raw and angry was instrumental in bringing about change. It brought out perspectives that had never been aired before and led to new insights.

The important question to ask yourself is what you will do and what you will not do when you face angry and indignant responses to conversations around diversity. You need to work that out ahead of time because you are not likely to be well equipped to deal with it in the moment. Preparing yourself in advance for such an event will help you to face it without reacting or going into problem-solving mode and, most importantly, not taking strong reactions personally.

Diversity is an emotive subject and if you open up conversations in a hitherto closed culture, expect a wellspring of frustrations to come to the surface. It's important at this point to not personalise or become defensive. These issues didn't start with you, they won't end with you. Of course, own up to and acknowledge any behaviours and sleights you are accused of that you know have some truth in them, but mostly your job is to listen and understand. You need to put your ego aside – that part of your mind which believes it is the centre of the universe and everything is about you. The ego always wants to be right and will move to defend itself if it feels attacked. It's part of being human, but so is transcending the ego and deepening human connections by listening and seeing how much of the universe exists outside of yourself.

If you are in a situation where uncomfortable truths are emerging, remember to breathe. Use a 4-5-6 breathing method: breathe in through the nose for four seconds, hold for five seconds and then out through the mouth for six seconds. This will help to lower tension and keep you in the present moment. A silent phrase such as this Buddhist mantra can help to keep you grounded and stop the ego from going into autodrive: 'I want everything for you and nothing from you.' Repeat it as you breathe and listen, and I can guarantee two things will occur. First, the angry person will calm down, as their anger has nowhere to go when they feel listened to. Second, you will learn things about yourself and your people which will surprise and enlighten you.

Summary

Open enquiry is a key method that you can use to build bridges, strengthen relationships and learn new insights about your employees and teams. You will also learn much about yourself. While the last chapter dealt with your own exclusion stories, this chapter has been about honing the skills to learn how others have experienced exclusion and the impact it has had on their lives. In seeking first to understand and then to be understood, you will learn about what is happening in the lives of your people.

Some of the skills in open enquiry may be strong in you and others you may need to practise. Listening to someone else with all your senses is surprisingly demanding. Settling your mind, body and energy to be receptive to others can be a challenge. Uncomfortable conversations may arise as you hear and meet with truths and realities that are different from your own. Your challenge, should you choose to accept it, is to go through that discomfort, sit in the difficult conversations and get to the light of understanding at the other end.

SUGGESTED EXERCISES

1. Introduce round-robin openers to your meetings where you ask each person 'What is going on in your world?', allowing them a few minutes to answer. This will start an attitude of listening and learning about each other.

2. Practise the skills of open enquiry with someone you know and trust. Get feedback on how you can improve and hone your skills and when you feel ready, start to apply them in work situations.

9
Nourish Green Shoots

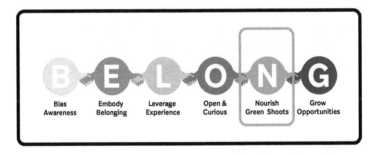

Now you understand the value of your own experiences of exclusion and how to learn about others', you can turn your attention to developing activities and initiatives that will nourish and grow a culture of belonging. You can build on those that have already been developed in your organisation and create new ones that will help your division, your teams and your direct reports. This is a time to take initiative, take risks and be creative.

Change happens through action, so the changes you make now will cause big shifts in your culture, and this is where many organisations get stuck. After the initial excitement of launching its DE&I strategy and initiatives, the central machine slows down and looks to you, the leaders, to take up the mantle and make things happen. As we know, sometimes things don't happen because many leaders feel uncertain and unsure about what to do from here, but if you have followed the ideas in this book so far and are ready to act on them, this won't be your experience. You will be primed and ready to make a big difference in how you lead and how others follow you. If you have opened up conversations with your immediate reports, with their teams and in larger forums, then you will already see some green shoots of change. Now is the time to nourish them and watch them grow.

The arc of change

In creating a culture of belonging, you are embarking on a significant change journey. As a business leader, you will know the ups and downs of change and it is even more difficult when we want to change attitudes and behaviours. We have to appeal in a different way to our employees if we want them to go on that journey with us.

Based on the work by Elisabeth Kübler-Ross, in explaining grief, the idea that we go through emotional stages when we face big changes in our life was later popularised in business.[43] It is often presented as a dip, like on a rollercoaster, as your emotions plumet and then find a way of building back up again. The five stages as defined in the change curve are:

1. Shock which often comes out as denial

2. Anger which transforms to depression

3. Reflection which is also seen as a time of exploring, both the change and what it means

4. Acceptance, coming to terms with the changed world

5. Exploring how life will change with the new reality

As social and emotional beings, we display predictable patterns of behaviour when we face challenges in life. I refer to the change curve in my strategy work or in my seminars, to highlight the emotional journey of change we all go through, but many leaders ignore this. They want to set new ways of working and new rules, and expect their people to just get on with it. They are genuinely surprised at the slump in productivity when their big idea fails to launch.

Our emotions are part of our processing centre as we navigate change. All of us have spikes of resistance when we are experiencing something new. In business, we don't talk about emotions at all, which is a missed opportunity. Our emotions will determine our thinking, our thinking will determine our actions and our actions will determine our performance. This is not about becoming an agony aunt or uncle to everyone in the company or trying to solve all the life problems your people might throw at you – there are plenty of places to get help for the deep stuff that people may be carrying – but if you are serious about creating a culture of belonging, you will allow more time for the daily emotional rollercoasters that your employees will likely be experiencing to be processed. You may have to work at being more articulate about your own emotions, as this will enable you to be comfortable when people are expressing theirs. People who rarely express emotions are nervous about having to deal with emotions from others. The more emotionally articulate you are, the easier it will become.

As leader, you are not immune to the effects of the change curve. The faster you and your people managers work through the curve, the easier it becomes to guide staff through the process. Two vital ingredients are information and conversation. When we understand what is happening and can talk through the implications and what we need to do differently, we come to acceptance quicker. Creating a culture of belonging is a major change and will challenge you and your staff. Some people will see it as positive and others will feel sidelined or threatened. Not everyone sees an upside and you need to be ready for it. As you hit pockets of resistance, drawing on the tools from the BELONG model will lessen the effects of the change curve. This is when your two-way dialogue, open enquiry and self-disclosure will help to bring your people on the DE&I journey and move through the change with minimised resistance.

Embrace diversity and learn from each other

There are many steps you can take to help nourish the green shoots of change, and your organisation may already have activities and events that you can get involved with. One growing trend in many organisations is the development of employee resource groups or affinity groups. This covers a wide range of areas, including women, black/multicultural groups, LGBTQ+ and neurodiversity. If you don't identify with a particular group, it might not be appropriate for you to be a member, but it might be possible to be a sponsor or guest at one of their meetings. You can share your own commitment to DE&I, what is happening in your area and where you might need their help. You might even share your own exclusion story if appropriate. Or you might just listen to what is shared by members of the group. You could offer yourself as an ally if members need a listening ear or guidance on how to navigate their career. These actions are great examples of 'leaning in' – the practice of showing interest and support to another group.

Throughout the year different cultural events will be celebrated, such as International Women's Day, Black History Month and Pride Month, and your organisation is likely to have a range of activities going on that educate and inspire others. You could support these by offering to sponsor them, or host them, or be part of the panel on them. Your interest will lend weight and send powerful signals of your commitment to DE&I.

One of my client organisations, based in Ireland, had a diverse range of employees from across Europe and Asia. They held a monthly cultural lunch where one person would bring in a food or item or tradition and share that with the group. They would share how it is made, why it is important and how the food links to cultural traditions. After everyone had shared the food or item, there would be a Q & A about it. Everyone would finish by offering one word of praise or describing what they had learned from the lunch. It was an extremely uplifting event which everyone looked forward to. It cost nothing yet went a long way towards building bridges and raising awareness.

Could you celebrate diversity by holding similar events in your business? Are there people from your employee group or community that you could invite to share their experiences? Could you bring in local charities or community groups to share the work they do with disadvantaged groups and the issues that their clients face? Two areas that get little attention but will affect up to 10% of your workforce are survivors of domestic abuse and care leavers. Both are disadvantaged when entering the workplace but are often overlooked or their needs ignored. There are many community groups supporting these populations that might come and do a talk with your employees to raise awareness of the issues their clients face and how best to support them in the workplace.

Building opportunities to celebrate diversity and learn from each other does not need to be costly or overly complicated – the easier and more relaxed the better – but it takes time and commitment on your part. As a leader, you have a greater influence on the actions of others. What you commit to will go a long way in determining what your people are prepared to commit to. Use the events that already exist in your organisation as a starting point but look at how you can organise more local events that engage, inform and inspire your employees to think differently and be more aware of the diverse needs of their colleagues and their community.

Build your network of DE&I ambassadors

If you have been part of any big transition or change programme (and which business leader hasn't?), you will remember how change champions helped to drive home the new ways of working. Sometimes they were in that role full time and their day job was backfilled, but mostly it was done alongside their day job. You can help reach out to all the different populations that you oversee by creating a network of DE&I ambassadors.

As you build momentum around local events, celebrations and talks, you will see those who are passionate about the cause and want to do more. These are your change ambassadors who can help spread the word and influence the organisation at a deeper level than you may reach. It is often the hourly population, shop floor or zero-hours contractors that are the hardest to reach as they are working different hours, or in more remote settings; or perhaps they come from a community where English is not the first language. Corporate programmes can be notoriously difficult in getting to these 'hard to reach' populations and yours might be no different. There may be pockets of workers in your own division that are difficult to access through your traditional communication channels. Developing a network of enthusiastic supporters of DE&I across your teams will help to reach these employees in a way that formal approaches will not.

Another effective approach is to define special projects that volunteers can work on to solve a particular issue. One of my clients had limited dedicated resources for DE&I, so after defining the priorities for the year, they created special projects. These included finding innovative ways to get participation from hourly workers in the affinity groups, or piloting a reverse mentoring scheme (see Chapter 5) or helping to design a DE&I award scheme.

Think about what reward or recognition would come from being an ambassador or taking up a special project before you launch it. For many of the individuals who apply, there is the intrinsic award of being singled out, having more visibility and doing something that is more challenging and worthwhile to support their colleagues, but that will not be the case for everyone, nor is it enough to keep the momentum going. The rewards do not have to have a large budget attached to them; they can be in the form of greater weighting of goals at end-year reviews, spot bonuses or a DE&I award ceremony with some nominal cash prize attached.

Once you are ready to launch your DE&I ambassadors, build their work into your own priorities to ensure it gets the attention it deserves. One thing that these ambassadors should expect is regular face time with you. They can report on what they have achieved, what got in the way and what help they might need to break down organisational barriers. These are the meetings where you need to listen, using open enquiry, to understand and facilitate their thinking. You want your DE&I ambassadors to think on their feet, be creative and try new things rather than rely on you to come up with the answers.

Celebrate and share best practice

As soon as you see changes and benefits emerge from the efforts of your teams and DE&I ambassadors, it's time to share them, not only within your division, but across divisions. Put it on the agenda for your meetings with your CEO or your peer forums. Share insights, actions, benefits and business results. Share your own journey with DE&I and how you have learned to grow in confidence through your actions. Offer yourself as a resource for other leaders to learn from. Be an ally for your peers as they start the journey. In your division, look at how to celebrate and share best practice. Could you have sessions in your management forums where you bring along a DE&I ambassador to highlight the work and results they have achieved? Perhaps an outside speaker could be invited to discuss their experiences of building inclusion and belonging in the workplace?

Awards can be a great motivator and a good way of highlighting innovative work. You could create a DE&I award, or a joint values/DE&I award process where end-year celebrations name those who have gone above and beyond in finding creative ways to build a culture of belonging. The more you can showcase the great work going on by highlighting it at important events such as management meetings, team meetings, town halls and fireside chats, the more you will inspire and encourage your employees to find better ways of being inclusive. As the green shoots of change emerge, use your influence to nurture them and clearly signpost how important the work is.

Special projects and community awareness

A final area that can reap great rewards and educate your employees on the many ways that diversity shows up is community projects. Think about what you can do within your division to encourage more community participation, and look at what you can leverage from existing initiatives for your teams. Your organisation may already have a policy to allow for paid time off to support agreed causes. If such a policy does not exist then consider creating one for your area, or find flexibility in work duties to allow for community-based work. There are so many causes out there that will help your employees appreciate areas such as personal trauma, physical and mental disabilities, poverty and abuse.

It can be even more powerful if you link your business to a cause. A food business could partner with charities tackling poor child nutrition, a fashion brand could partner with domestic abuse charities, or a pharmaceutical company could partner with drug addiction charities. When you have a charity of choice, find out what they need from you and how you can help. Often, that falls into several categories:

- Fundraising or sponsorship of events

- Supporting projects such as helping to build a play area or redecorate a children's ward

- Offering advice by coming in and helping to solve a strategic problem

- Volunteering to do work with the charity to help their agreed client group

You could consider becoming a trustee of a local charity. This is a personal commitment made in your own time, where you help steer the charity, shape its strategy and give advice on its day-to-day running. You would bring many valuable skills to the table while becoming educated on the needs of a disadvantaged group.

Summary

Nourishing green shoots is about taking action to tip the diversity scales in the right direction. This requires focus and effort. You will experience the challenges that come with change while you are supporting others through it as well. As a leader, you are experienced in navigating change, but this time may feel more personal than other business initiatives, because it requires so much from you. Be aware of this and how the change curve may affect you as you go through the journey. Expect the dip in the curve and the bad days, but find the support you need to get through them.

There are many activities that you could consider in nourishing green shoots, including hosting or supporting affinity groups, supporting local community groups or developing a network of DE&I ambassadors in your workplace. The most important thing is to do something and share the benefits widely across your organisation to inspire others. This is how green shoots become a burgeoning harvest of initiatives and momentum in creating a culture of belonging.

SUGGESTED EXERCISES

1. Consider building a network of enthusiastic people who represent all areas of your organisation to champion DE&I, lead lunch-and-learns and set up smaller local activities to help bring people on the journey. See further resources at the back of this book for a suggested job description.

2. Look at how you and your teams can get involved with local community groups supporting diverse or minority populations.

10

Grow Opportunities

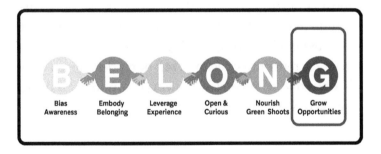

Bias Awareness · **Embody Belonging** · **Leverage Experience** · **Open & Curious** · **Nourish Green Shoots** · **Grow Opportunities**

If you have got to this stage and followed through the actions of the previous steps of the BELONG model, you will have already seen some significant changes not only in how you work, but in how your people feel about working for you. This is a great foundation from which to grow opportunities for under-represented groups. The last step of the BELONG model is about using the data and information available to you to decide on what action to take.

In modern organisations, data is the lifeblood of decisions. You will have data on almost everything you need at the touch of a button, but data is deeply flawed, as it only tells the story we have asked for. The reason data results are so often skewed is that we have not asked the right questions. This will be true when you think of minority populations in your organisation. Data on ethnic or racial identity is often not available, and how can you know if you have a bias in your recruitment and employment without it? This is a question that many businesses around the world are asking themselves. With the exception of the USA, most countries, particularly across Europe, only collect data on gender systematically. You need to look at creative methods of gathering and analysing data on your current employee mix, but don't despair, as data is only one of several ways you can understand the needs of your minority groups.

Use data to understand the size of the problem

You use data every day to make decisions. Data about finance, performance, market conditions and even your smart watch data to monitor your health. Data is everywhere, and that is also true of the data used to uncover the inequalities that exist within your own workforce. The first place to look will be in the self-service reports within the HR system. Start by collecting data on the characteristics that are built into the system, such as gender, age, tenure, level. You may also collect data on race and ethnicity, but that may be patchy as not all geographies capture this.

You could layer other data such as engagement scores or any other employee survey, completion of DE&I training and performance scores. The latter are particularly insightful if you cut them by population (age, gender, tenure). This might be a little more data crunching and you may need a data analyst to help produce the graphs to show correlations which become your dashboard. If you have a small team, it might only be one dashboard. If you have a large and complex structure, it might be cut by division or geography. The data will help you see patterns and gaps and this allows for questions to be raised, such as:

- Where might we have implicit bias in our recruitment processes?

- Are we seeing a trend of our female employees feeling less engaged than our male colleagues and why?

- Does our employee population fairly reflect the ethnic and racial profile of our wider community?

- Does tenure differ by gender or race?

- Is the uptake of DE&I training evenly spread across all populations?

- Have the promotions over the last twelve to twenty-four months had a pattern that would suggest unconscious bias?

- Do we have any activities to support diverse or minority-owned suppliers?

The more you engage with the data, the more questions will arise that will lead to new insights. Change occurs with insights, so the more you understand the size and nature of the barriers that exist, the more effective the solution will be. I will share the story of what one leader found when he started digging into the data.

CHANGING THE RECRUITMENT PROCESS

Peter, a leader in a technology group, raised questions about why there was not enough diversity in his teams, particularly in some pockets where the community was diverse, but the workforce was almost entirely white. After attending some DE&I workshops and then looking at his own data, he saw a strong pattern of bias in the recruitment process. When he spoke to recruiters and headhunters, they said they could never find enough black or female candidates who were qualified or educated enough for these roles. This felt wrong to him.

Peter brought all of his hiring managers together and asked them to commit to having a diverse candidate slate for all interviews. They brought in a team to look at all job descriptions. Any gender or racial bias was identified and changed.

Peter worked with the talent acquisition team and his hiring managers to agree what a diverse slate would look like and how recruitment should be conducted and where. He also agreed to manage business challenges should the recruitment process to bring more diverse talent take longer.

Within six months, there was a considerable change in the profile of new joiners. While the overall population was still out of kilter with the population profile in the community, the new employees were more diverse and came from many different backgrounds.

Bias-busting clinics – a safe place to learn together

Even using the method of data collection, pilot, test and report described above, you will need to gather information from other sources. In Chapter 8, we covered how to stay open and curious and go to the network meetings or open up conversations in your own team forums to understand what is going on behind the scenes. Your efforts should not stop there. If you can see the data pointing to an issue, but you cannot explain it, consider holding one-off focus groups or bias-busting clinics where you invite people from the affected population to a discussion.

Using an external facilitator to hold such an event will encourage more open discussion. Most of the employees in these groups will have faced discrimination their whole life and this may be the first time they have ever been asked to describe it. That can lead to a wellspring of emotional outpouring which reflects that wider arc of experience, not just how people have been treated in your organisation. Be sensitive to the context in which feedback is given. Perception is one person's reality, so even if this does not fully reflect the reality for many in your organisation, give due respect and consideration to everything you hear.

A UK-based professional services firm commissioned us to hold focus groups to see where their DE&I strategies were failing to land well. A number of major themes came through the discussions. While great efforts had been made to identify diverse candidates (particularly care leavers) for intern roles, there was still strong evidence of the old-boy network among partners. Children of partners with private education were often taken on without interview, as opposed to the heavy assessment days that other interns had to go through.

The tone that partners adopted with junior staff failed to take into account different economic realities of their working-class and usually under-represented employees. Starting conversations about skiing holidays, golf days or even which private club they belonged to created an obvious gulf between senior and junior members of the team. The information was brought to partners of the firm, and further support and coaching in DE&I was organised to help them to minimise the sense of difference between their experiences and that of their employees.

Bias-busting clinics can reveal issues that would not easily come to the fore through surveys or team events. After you have gathered data and drawn some conclusions, share the outcomes with all of those who contributed to the review. This makes people feel that their opinion matters and that they can have confidence that the organisation is listening to them.

Challenge the status quo

One of the best ways to challenge the status quo is by having external guests who can tell their story in a compelling and enlightening way. Hearing first-hand the challenges a person who comes from a minority has faced can have a big impact. I remember one disabled rights campaigner who was brought in to speak at an employee forum. She relied on an electric wheelchair for mobility and it had not been easy to access the building or to find the right space for her to do her talk. This spoke volumes. Exclusion for her started at the front door and she did not shy away from explaining the daily indignities she suffered, simply because buildings were not accessible to her. The company she had been invited to speak to was only in its early days of embracing diversity, and they learned a salutary lesson in how much more thinking needed to go into their workplace. This speaker did more in a one-hour conversation to raise awareness and challenge thinking than had been achieved in the previous nine months of activity. By embodying the exclusion that the training, policies and initiatives were trying to redress, her presence brought the issues to life.

I often provide talks to affinity groups that cover many areas of diversity, gender and intersectionality. One of my most popular stories is my experience as a woman in a man's world. I had been the chief executive of a regional charity for five years, in a majority female organisation that provided social care to adults with autism, when I felt ready to move into management consultancy. I was still a young and ambitious leader when I joined a large and predominantly male management consultancy. Many of the consultants treated me and my background with derision, feeling that I would know nothing about the world of business. When new projects came up, I was often overlooked, even though I had availability. In meetings I was ignored or patronised for my view, being told I didn't know how real consultancy was done.

It was a difficult time in my career and I seriously questioned if I had made the right decision. Things changed for me when I won work on my own merit and was able to land some big clients for the firm. I was aware that I had to adapt my style to this harder and more competitive environment, yet find a way to do it with my own values intact. This helped me to be more specific in what type of consultancy I wanted to do and what type of organisation I wanted to do it with, and I used my experiences with this firm as a lesson in what I was looking for in my next employer.

There are many good organisations out there who have engaging guest speakers who will help to challenge the status quo through the power of sharing their stories of overcoming adversity.

Set and share priority areas

Like Peter, the leader in the technology group, you need to think about which areas you want to make a priority and then set some goals around them. If the data is telling you the issues are in recruitment or in retention, get a working group together to investigate what might be the root cause of the issue. A 5 Whys exercise can be helpful for getting to the root cause.

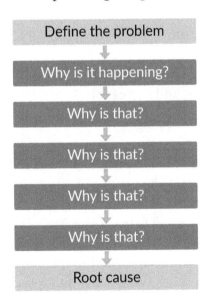

The 5 Whys

The 5 Whys technique was created in the 1930s by Sakichi Toyoda, the Japanese industrialist, inventor and founder of Toyota Industries. It became popular in the 1970s and is a widely used management tool today. It's a simple yet powerful exercise. Each 'why' should lead to different insights that help to get to the core issues. This will often entail some further data collection, so expect a working group to take between two and four weeks to get to some meaningful insights that they can share with you. Once you have these, together with your DE&I dashboard and feedback from your DE&I ambassadors, you should have several data points that help you work out your priority areas. The most common DE&I priorities tend to be:

- Recruitment

- Retention (or regrettable leavers)

- Promotion and succession

- Awareness raising

Decide which one is a priority for you and your direct reports. Explain the result you are looking for, then ask the working team to come up with the initiatives that will help to get to that result. Whatever the agreed action, a baseline should be set at the outset and all of your teams then expected to follow the new ways of working. A time frame should be set for the new policy to take hold and then a review and measure of the benefits should be undertaken at the end of the agreed pilot period.

By taking a disciplined approach to using the data that is at hand as well as reliable data collection methods, you use evidence to support your DE&I activities. The results and benefits can be shared across the organisation. In this way, you are not only solving the issues for your own division but helping the entire group to create a culture of belonging.

Summary

Growing opportunities for minorities requires a multipronged data-driven approach. First, we need awareness of the need to grow these opportunities. Then, we need to know the size of the problem. We do this through asking pertinent questions, gathering the data and putting resources together that can help to work through the issues and identify meaningful interventions.

You can enhance your reach in the organisation by developing a network of DE&I ambassadors, who are not only your eyes and ears into your employee populations that are hard to reach, but also help to shape interventions that will enhance the culture of belonging.

Taking a disciplined approach to defining root causes of the DE&I issues and assigning resources to solve problems will bring meaningful benefits that can be shared with your peer group and across your organisation.

SUGGESTED EXERCISES

1. Build a dashboard that gives you a split of your organisation by gender and by race/ethnicity, and then split by team, by region, by level. Layer on data that helps you to understand some underlying trends like turnover by gender and leadership levels by race etc. Use this dashboard to lead conversations with your direct reports on how to improve diversity and belonging in your teams.

2. Consider going further by having bias-busting clinics – one-off focus groups that bring people from different backgrounds together to consider some of the big questions (or gaps) arising from the data to hand.

3. Based on your new insights, set some clear DE&I priorities that you will be held accountable for.

PART THREE
MAKING CHANGE STICK

11
Organisational Levers

Now that we have covered the BELONG model and what the six steps entail, we can move on to discussing how to implement this and sustain momentum over time. We have talked about the organisational levers you can pull throughout this book, as it's important to remember you are not on this journey alone. Your organisation is likely to have several DE&I initiatives underway, and you will get further and have greater impact if your actions, efforts and priorities are in concert with the overall direction.

Start by speaking to the head of DE&I or the team that supports this area. Find out what they are doing, see where you can help and if they need somewhere to pilot new ideas, then be the first to volunteer. By being ready, willing and able to lean into the subject, you will already be ahead of many leaders in your organisation and you will benefit from the support available to you.

Use these levers to build the foundations for your own DE&I initiatives. Look beyond the boundaries of your organisation to the many forums and organisations out there that can offer a wider perspective. The wider you reach, the more innovative and original your thinking will become. A great way to determine how far you are on the journey and what you can do to progress is with a benchmark. There is already a global standard for this that you can use, and it is a free and readily available resource.

The Global Diversity, Equity and Inclusion Benchmarks

One of the most respected and trusted measures of DE&I are the Global Diversity, Equity and Inclusion Benchmarks (GDEIB), which were developed by The Centre for Global Inclusion. This is a free resource that has standards across fifteen areas, as illustrated by the image below.

Foundation *Drive the Strategy*	Bridging *Align & Connect*
1. Vision Strategy and Business Impact	8. Assessment Measurement and Research
2. Leadership and Accountability	9. DEI Communications
3. DEI Structure and Implementation	10. DEI Learning and Development
	11. Connecting DEI and Sustainability
Internal *Attract & Retain People*	**External** *Listen To & Serve Society*
4. Recruitment	12. Community Government Relations and Philanthropy
5. Advancement and Retention	13. Services and Product Development
6. Job Design Classifcation and Compensation	14. Marketing and Customer Service
7. Work-Life Integration Flexibility and Benefits	15. Responsible Sourcing

The Global Diversity, Equity and Inclusion Benchmarks[44]

While most of the measures are from an organisational perspective and you may not be able to influence them, there are some you can shape, such as decisions around recruitment, development, promotion and leadership behaviours. Look at the four key categories, review the ones that you feel you can directly influence and look at what action can be taken. If they become part of your personal commitments and priorities, remember to share this with your immediate reports and your wider teams, because if they understand your priorities, they will make them theirs. Build your priorities into your regular management updates and share them with your directors and peers. Make it obvious that they are part of your commitments and that you hold them in equal value to other business objectives.

The benchmark exercise is something that you or a member of your team could easily do. You will be able to answer most of the indicators with a simple yes or no: you either have them in place or you don't. You can use the benchmark as a yearly exercise to check in with where you are doing well. Are you seeing the needle move and is there good news to share? This is great for engaging employees in the journey and sharing the progress you have made towards creating a culture of belonging.

The GDEIB have five levels:

- Level 1 – Passive
- Level 2 – Reactive

- Level 3 – Proactive

- Level 4 – Progressive

- Level 5 – Best practice

When they first come to the process, most organisations find themselves at Level 1, with some activities bringing them to Level 2. Don't be disheartened if you start at a low level. If you apply the techniques and launch the activities from the BELONG model, you will compile evidence over a year or two that will move you up the scale. A good target to set would be to achieve Level 3 within two years. To get beyond that, the whole organisation needs to be aligned around its DE&I priorities, in a position to pull the structural and process levers.

It's important not to do this journey alone. You have people within your HR function or perhaps a DE&I team who you can draw on for support, inspiration and practical tools, but don't stop there. There are many industry leaders you could approach who would be a great source of further help. The Centre for Global Inclusion, which is behind the global benchmark, has a list of sponsors and there may be organisations worth talking to.

Consider your near competitors. Do they have a DE&I web page and do they report on progress annually? If so, they might offer insights into what has worked for them. It is worth contacting not only the head of

DE&I in these organisations, but your counterpart as well. Get a view from the business leaders of what has helped them and where they still find things challenging. It might provide opportunities to collaborate and benefit both of your organisations.

External networks

Another important source of inspiration as you develop your DE&I priorities and launch actions will be networks of like-minded professionals. Networking is a great way to refresh your thinking, find new and innovative ideas and meet people who can be useful to you, your team and your organisation. There are a range of DE&I events throughout the year that you can attend to learn more about the subject, meet interesting speakers worth inviting to your own events and get support from people who have been there.

A good place to start would be your own professional bodies. Look at the events they are holding and make a commitment to go to one or two each year that will support your DE&I efforts. If they are not holding such events, then perhaps as a member you could lobby them to do so. Your voice matters and they will welcome your suggestions. Beyond this, there are a range of other professional networks out there. For example, the UK-based d&i Leaders Forum meets two or three times a year and has several flagship events. Although it is often geared towards those holding the role of DE&I leader, that does not preclude interested and active business leaders like yourself.

Through these events, you will hear up-to-date thinking and research about DE&I. Networking will help you be more confident with your own efforts and actions. Seeing and hearing what other people are doing can be a real confidence boost when you realise that you have already made inroads into the area. You will see how your early efforts can grow into great things that shift the culture, and you will provide inspiration for other people both in your organisation and beyond it. The more you share your story, your journey and your learning, the more you inspire other leaders to do the same.

Access great behaviour-based training

Much of *The Inclusion Edge* has been about what you can do to change the culture of your organisation. You hold an important role in creating a culture of belonging, but you are not on this journey alone and you should use the resources that are available within and beyond your company. Start with the curriculums already in place. Are there online modules available that help with addressing bias and fostering inclusion? If not, raise the question with your training team. Find out if this is on a roadmap, or if they have a budget for you to bring in resources.

External resources found through networking will also be a great place to ask questions about the type of training they provide their employees and who they recommend. You often need a multi-tiered approach to your training. Facilitated workshops and discussions with your direct reports helps to prepare them to lead out on discussions with their teams. People leaders might want some tailored modules to help them address any bias in how they manage their teams. These could be a mixture of instructor-led or online events. Your employees could access training in fostering inclusion, which gives them tips and skills they can take away and apply. Online training, delivered in local languages, is often an effective way to get this through the ranks.

If you have or are rolling out this training, think about how you can create incentives and recognise attendance and behavioural outcomes. Could it be an objective for all employees to attend at least one training module or perhaps have a badge on their profile recognising they have completed the course? Would it be worth linking the training to the idea of a DE&I award process where significant changes in the workplace are recognised? Think about how you link the training to business outcomes you want to achieve (for example, engagement scores) and whether rewards for employees and teams could be linked to their training and behaviour change efforts. Training alone will not effect change, but the reinforcement that follows it will. The best way to ensure that people do things differently is to give them an incentive to do so. Post-training incentives and recognition are an effective way to achieve this.

Address bias in your talent processes

Does bias exist in your talent processes? You would hope that the answer is no, but in reality, it usually does. Bias shows up in many ways. Start with the recruitment process, or talent acquisition, and look at the job descriptions for five jobs in your division. Does the language of that job description appeal more to men or women? There are websites which you can use to upload the text and see if there is an implicit bias. One such tool is Textio: www.textio.com.

What about job expectations? Post-Covid, our view of the balance between office and home working has changed, but do the expectations of the job assume full office attendance and lots of travel? Are these realistic or are they historically what has been expected? Female talent may not apply for roles that imply a lack of flexibility. Does that matter to you? If it does, then you need to revisit the expectations of the role.

There's a saying about diversity that is a useful guide: 'If you can't see it, you can't be it!' Think about your interview panels. Are they all male? All white? All over forty? If you want diverse talent to be attracted to your organisation, they need to see this in their first interactions with you. The interview panel should be as diverse as possible, and diversity should come from within the ranks. If that is genuinely not possible, can you organise some sort of gathering where interviewees meet employees from a range of backgrounds? Raise the potential of your diverse talent by showing a commitment to seeing it in action.

What about a high-potential programme? Does your organisation single out young talent with the potential for leadership roles and fast-track their career? This is common in many global organisations and is a good place to look at where there may be some bias. What is the spread of population in terms of gender, race, education and geography? Does it accurately reflect your employee population or the communities you serve? If you see that there is a bias towards, for example, males or elite educational institutions, is there something you can do to address this?

Bias also shows up in promotion processes. Look at the promotions across your division over the last twenty-four months. Is there a pattern emerging? Are you seeing evenly spread promotions based on gender? What about geography? Do you see promotions occurring more for those who are in headquarters than those from regional offices? Race also needs to be considered. Based on the percentage of black and ethnic minority employees, how consistently do they get promoted versus your white population?

If you see that white males tend to progress at a faster rate than other employees, then you need to look at the root causes. These may include not only the competency models and assumptions about leadership, but also who is in the room making decisions about promotion. If the decisions around promotion are made by people who are perpetuating a certain type of leader, this needs to be challenged. We all tend to like people like us and overidentify with them. Leaders are no different.

Summary

This chapter focused on what is readily available to support your DE&I work. A great place to start is by looking at what your organisation has already put in place, that you can use within your own teams and reporting lines. Benchmarking is great for knowing where you are and how far you have to go and this work has already been done by The Centre for Global Inclusion.

Getting advice and inspiration from beyond your organisation will also help. Use your own networks or look to competitors who are already front runners in terms of DE&I to gain ideas. You will find that they are more than willing to share their DE&I work.

You can also access many resources in your organisation that will help you, such as behaviour-based training and resource groups, so these should not be overlooked.

SUGGESTED EXERCISES

1. Download the GDEIB from The Centre for Global Inclusion. Study the standards and make a list of those you would like to prioritise. Access the benchmarks here: www.centreforglobalinclusion. org.

2. Investigate and attend networking events around DE&I, either through your industry, professional bodies or through the d&I Leaders Global Forum: www.dileaders.com/globalforum.

12
Commit To Action

We are held accountable for our goals when we share them with others and make a commitment to achieve them. The BELONG model gives guidance on what you might set as your DE&I priorities. The wider you share your commitments, the more likely you are to complete them. With so many other competing priorities, this step is crucial if you are to maintain momentum beyond your initial actions and bring your people on the DE&I journey. Now is the time to be bold, be ambitious and be challenging in the goals that you set for yourself, thereby setting the bar higher for everyone else.

Create and share your own DE&I manifesto

There is no accountability like public accountability, so if you are serious about DE&I and creating a culture of belonging, it's time to define your manifesto. By this stage, you will have already given serious thought to your commitments and taken some action towards getting comfortable with the subject, so now you just need to let everyone know what you are doing and are going to keep doing to help further the efforts of DE&I and create equity in your division and organisation. Your goals could cover, for example:

- **Gender equity goals:** What targets will you set for gender representation at the non-manager and line manager levels in your division? What expectations do you have about the gender split of your immediate reports? Put a time frame on achievement. If you have a low base (less than 30% female) you will need at least five years to see changes, otherwise the churn might cause too much business disruption. If you have a higher base, then you might set a more challenging time frame.

- **Race/ethnicity goals:** Starting with your base and the percentage split in the general population of your community, is there a gap? Think of your goals across both non-manager and manager populations. Think in terms of three- to five-year time frames.

- **Training:** Set targets for training uptake for all employees in your division. Also set some goals on what additional training/mentoring/reverse mentoring/sponsoring you are going to do across the year.

- **Events:** Celebrating Black History Month, International Women's Day and Pride should feature in your manifesto. Don't try to cover every feast, celebration or religious observation, but try to cover those that are important to your employee population. If you have a particular ethnic or religious group, then honour and represent their celebrations sensitively.

- **Sponsorship:** This might be linked to a programme that your organisation already has in place, in which case you are making a personal commitment within an identified scheme to sponsor one or two people. If your organisation does not have one, then develop a sponsorship scheme that helps emerging talent and gives them advice and support when they need it. Your commitments might be to set up a sponsorship scheme and then set a goal for how many people will be identified and sponsored through the year.

- **Authenticity:** The final goal would be a deeply personal one around how you show up every day in an open, honest and approachable way. Think about what would be most demonstrable for you and offer that up as your authenticity goal.

By making DE&I integral to your business priorities you will ensure that it gets the attention it deserves and send out a powerful message to all your people that you are committed to achieving equality and belonging at work. When you have defined all these goals they become your DE&I manifesto – your public declaration of priorities and goals to create a culture of belonging. When you have your manifesto, get it printed and display it in your office. Share it with your direct reports and with your teams. Let them know why this is important to you and how you intend to stick to it. Ask for their help in reminding you if they believe you are slipping. You will find a template at the back of this book and this is also available at: www.agents2change.com/theinclusionedge.

Set stretching DE&I goals for you and your team

You need to bring your people with you on your DE&I journey and nothing drives behaviour quite like goals. Alongside the business goals that you will already have in place, add some that mirror the expectations of your manifesto. For your direct reports, setting generic representation targets won't make sense, so you will need to make them contextual to their environment and processes.

You may have different issues around training attendance. If you have a mixture of office-based and hourly workers, then access to training will differ and their own training goals, such as timescale and percentage completion, should reflect their needs. Ask for a personal commitment from each team member – you could do this through your DE&I ambassador network. When everyone has identified their goals, these should be printed and displayed alongside yours and also shared with their immediate reports and cascaded through the ranks. The more public these commitments are, the more impact they will have in changing the culture.

Start with one clear priority

You now have a range of behavioural interventions for yourself and your team. You may even have published your DE&I manifesto. This is great, but now what? Implementation is about systematically turning these goals into action. While you might have five or six key priorities for DE&I which sit alongside other business priorities, you only have so much bandwidth and you need to get traction on some of these goals to move them forward.

For your DE&I goals, start with one clear priority. Based on, for example, your representation goals, where do you need to invest the most time and effort? Often, this is in the recruitment process. What project and plan could be put together to look at that? What resources do you need to gather from inside your own organisation and by partnering with HR that can help you define the brief and put a plan together? Set clear expectations and a time frame, then allocate the resources to do the work. Once you have a team up and running to look at the issue, make sure you find time to meet with them regularly. You do not want to set them adrift, because once it stops being a priority for you, it will stop being a priority for them.

When you have the first big initiative underway, move on to the next one. By the end of the year, you might have two or three projects that have been set up in this way and have made significant inroads into addressing organisational and structural barriers for diverse populations.

Summary

In this chapter, you are publicly stating your commitments to DE&I. This brings accountability and transparency. Your DE&I manifesto will set the tone and expectations for everyone who works for you, and from this manifesto, you will determine the right goals to set for your immediate reports, who will in turn cascade them to their teams.

When you have defined what these are, it's best to start with one clear priority as the initial theme. This does not mean that the other areas will be ignored, only that your time and the deeper analysis will go to solving one issue at a time.

SUGGESTED EXERCISES

1. Define your commitments and priority areas for DE&I. When you are happy with these, share them with your direct reports and get their feedback.

2. Draw up a DE&I manifesto to define what your personal commitments will be. When you are happy with it, share it widely. A DE&I manifesto template can be found at the back of this book or downloaded from www.agents2change.com/theinclusionedge.

Conclusion

Now you have set out your priorities and created your personal manifesto, it all comes down to action. You know that change can only happen through action, so now is the time to focus on timelines, actions and the resources you will need to achieve that change. You need to build the plan and put the team together to make it happen.

Planning is likely to be second nature to you. Most of your time is probably spent setting objectives for others and then monitoring their progress and course-correcting when issues arise. Treat your DE&I work like any big initiative that you are overseeing. After all, that is what it is. This is about a change of culture and how work gets done and, as with any action, it requires a time frame and a desired end state that can be measured and reviewed regularly. Without this, it will not get the priority it deserves in your busy schedule and will lose momentum.

Build out your project plan. Start with a twelve-month period and decide what is going to be done, by who and by when. The plan will probably be in four main categories:

- **Self-development:** Honing and practising new skills and behaviours

- **Team development:** Introducing a range of interventions, including training, team building and workshops

- **Data development:** Gathering information to determine the effectiveness of your action and where attention is needed

- **Partnerships/collaborations:** Working with your talent teams, external bodies, benchmarking organisations, industry experts and coaches to help drive improvements

Organise the activity you are committing to in monthly or quarterly periods and outline what the end state will be. This might be a deliverable, such as an event or new policy, or a measure, such as training uptake or engagement scores.

Once you have the plan, share it with your immediate team and your boss. They need to be aware of it and why it is important. One or two of these deliverables will be baked into your own objectives, so they are central to your delivery. Share the plan with your peers to help them lead out on DE&I. Report progress at least quarterly. The monitoring and reporting stage is an important time to discuss where there are cultural or organisational barriers that need addressing. By bringing them up as part of an overall plan for DE&I, you raise awareness of these issues and focus your audience on problem-solving.

Gather support around you

By making your commitments public, you will also let your peers and your boss know how serious you are about this area. To be successful, you will need their support. Make sure the CEO is onboard and will support your efforts, as you want them to come to events, sponsor activities and even present DE&I awards. If you are the CEO, then seek the support of the chair or a board member.

Aim to give your peers a regular update about what's happening and what results you are seeing. These results might surprise you. Beyond some measures like engagement scores, expect to see some underlying changes, such as better attendance, lower staff turnover and improved morale. These can sometimes take time, but I have seen them turn around quickly when employees see their leaders are serious about DE&I.

Consider getting an accountability partner from outside of your organisation. Did you find an interesting person who would serve as a supporter when you were talking to your competitors or going to external events? If not, how about an external coach? An executive coach or a DE&I consultant can bring insight, challenge and guidance when you most need it. Having a coach allows you to share concerns and fears free of judgement. You can gain more meaningful insights when talking to someone who is removed from the situation but skilled at listening and playing back your thoughts. Your loved ones might also be an excellent support for you. A partner, a friend or even a parent can sometimes offer a view which differs greatly from how you or your organisation think and that can be helpful. If you are going to use them in this way, don't do it at random times, when you or they are perhaps under pressure or doing something important. Ask them if you can give them a weekly or monthly download and then set the time to do that, so there are clear boundaries between home and work life. Once you have finished your conversation, do not go back to it until the allotted time of the next session. This might sound formal for a friend or partner, but the boundaries are about respecting that they have a life and concerns of their own and they don't need to feel responsible for yours as well.

Celebrate success

Many organisations focus so much on planning and goals that they forget to celebrate success. This is not the way to keep your employees motivated. A celebration event does not need to be a big expensive affair. You will be surprised by how much impact even small gestures can make.

If you want people to stay on the DE&I journey with you, then reinforce the great work they are doing and the milestones they are achieving. Some ideas for how you can do this might include:

- **A dedicated DE&I award** with an annual or biannual ceremony. It could be a trophy (never underestimate the power of a trophy or plaque) and, if budget allows, a spot bonus or book voucher or cash voucher.

- **A shout-out email** to the one or the few that have been outstanding in their efforts in that period. This could be every week, every month or every quarter.

- **A 'take a break' reward** for a person or team which has achieved an important milestone, giving them a half-day off.

- **A handwritten thank-you note** from you, with or without a reward, to those who have been singled out for their exemplary service of DE&I.

The point is to do something. The gesture can be grand or small, but taking time to acknowledge the efforts of others will pay huge dividends. For more inspiration, see the additional resources section at the back of this book.

Your plan defines what DE&I will look like for yourself, your team and when partnering with others. Finding support from within and outside of your organisation will help you stay the distance as you hit the inevitable bumps in the road. Building in celebrations of success is a great motivator and is often missed or undervalued by organisations, so start thinking of what will work for your teams. Good luck and enjoy the journey.

If you have any comments or just want more inspiration, reach out to me at: mary@agents2change.com. You can also find more inspiration at: www.agents2change.com/theinclusionedge.

Notes

1 A Pandy, 'Why Did Blackberry Fail?' (Feedough, 2022),
   www.feedough.com/why-did-blackberry-fail, accessed
   30/07/22; C Mui, 'How Kodak Failed' (Forbes, 2012),
   www.forbes.com/sites/chunkamui/2012/01/18/how-
   kodak-failed, accessed 30/07/22; L Brinded, 'The Sorry
   History of the Near-Destruction of Investment Banking at
   RBS' (Insider, 2015), www.businessinsider.com/why-rbs-
   failed-as-an-investment-bank-2015-3?r=US&IR=T, accessed
   30/07/22
2 K Jacob et al, *Belonging* (Bloomsbury, 2020), p.xxiii
3 C Fulp, *Success Through Diversity: Why the most inclusive
   companies will win* (Beacon Press, 2018), p.34
4 V Hunt et al, *Delivering Through Diversity* (McKinsey,
   2018), www.mckinsey.com/business-functions/people-
   and-organizational-performance/our-insights/delivering-
   through-diversity, accessed 01/08/2022
5 R McGregor-Smith, *Race in the Workplace* (UK Government,
   2016), https://assets.publishing.service.gov.uk/
   government/uploads/system/uploads/attachment_data/
   file/594336/race-in-workplace-mcgregor-smith-review.pdf,
   accessed 29/08/2022

6 JT Kennedy, *What Majority Men Really Think About D&I* (Coqual, 2020), www.aiaa.org/docs/default-source/uploadedfiles/membership-and-communities/committees/majoritymenbelonging_report2-aug2020-cti.pdf, accessed 01/08/2022

7 S Frost, *The Inclusion Imperative: How real inclusion creates better business and builds better societies* (Kogan Page, 2014), pp.45–58

8 See endnote 7

9 M Williams, 'Embracing Change Through Inclusion: Meta's 2022 Diversity Report' (Meta, 19 July 2022), https://about.fb.com/news/2022/07/metas-diversity-report-2022, accessed 26/09/2022

10 See endnote 5

11 J Gifford, M Green, Jake Young and P Urwin, *Diversity Management That Works* (CIPD, 2019), www.cipd.co.uk/Images/7926-diversity-and-inclusion-report-revised_tcm18-65334.pdf, accessed 01/08/2022

12 US Equal Employment Opportunity Commission, 'Facts about Race/Color Discrimination' (1997), www.eeoc.gov/laws/guidance/facts-about-racecolor-discrimination, accessed 01/08/2022

13 R DiAngelo, *White Fragility* (Penguin, 2019)

14 S Helgesen and M Goldsmith, *How Women Rise: Break the 12 habits holding you back* (Random House, 2018), p.12

15 D Konigsburg and S Thorne, *Women in the Boardroom: A global perspective*, Seventh Edition (Deloitte, 2022), www2.deloitte.com/content/dam/Deloitte/global/Documents/gx-women-in-the-boardroom-seventh-edition.pdf, accessed 02/08/2022

16 T Burns et al, *Women in the Workplace 2021* (McKinsey and Company, 2021), www.mckinsey.com/featured-insights/diversity-and-inclusion/women-in-the-workplace, accessed 02/08/2022

17 M Parmelee and E Codd, *Women @ Work 2022: A global outlook* (Deloitte, 2022), www2.deloitte.com/content/dam/Deloitte/global/Documents/deloitte-women-at-work-2022-a-global-outlook.pdf, accessed 26/09/2022

18 T Chamorro-Premuzic, *Why Do So Many Incompetent Men Become Leaders?* (Harvard Business Review Press, 2019)

19 B Sears et al, *LGBT People's Experience of Workplace Discrimination and Harassment* (UCLA, 2021), https://

williamsinstitute.law.ucla.edu/publications/lgbt-workplace-discrimination, accessed 02/08/2022

20 See endnote 6

21 See endnote 6

22 E Hall, *Beyond Culture* (Anchor Books, 1997)

23 S Page, *The Diversity Bonus: How great teams pay off in the knowledge economy* (Princeton University Press, 2nd Edition, 2019)

24 A Maslow, 'A theory of human motivation', *Psychological Review*, 50/4 (1943), 370–96

25 MR Banaji and AG Greenwald, *Blindspot: Hidden biases of good people* (Delacorte Press, 2013), pp.123–144

26 C Jung, *The Undiscovered Self (Present and Future)* (Bollingen, 1959)

27 See endnote 24

28 C Rogers, *Client-Centered Therapy*, 70th Anniversary Edition (Robinson Publishing, 2003)

29 B Brown, *Rising Strong* (Vermilion, 2015), p.272

30 J Stavros et al, 'Appreciative Inquiry: Organization development and the strengths revolution', in *Practicing Organization Development: Leading transformation and change*, 4th Edition, pp.96–116 (Wiley Press, 2015)

31 See endnote 13

32 Infoplease, 'Major Religions of the World' (2021), www.infoplease.com/culture-entertainment/religion/major-religions-world, accessed 07/08/2022

33 B Looney, 'Diversity, Equity and Inclusion at bp' (2021), www.bpretailjobs.co.uk/life-at-bp, accessed 07/08/2022

34 D Zimmerman and C West, 'Sex roles, interruptions and silences in conversations', in *Language and Sex: Difference and dominance*, pp.105–129 (Stanford University Press, 1975), www.web.stanford.edu/~eckert/PDF/zimmermanwest1975.pdf, accessed 07/08/2022

35 D Tannen, *You Just Don't Understand: Women and men in conversation* (Virago, 1992), p.77

36 F Sheridan, 'Gender, language and the workplace: An exploratory study', *Women in Management Review*, 22/4 (2007), 319–336

37 T Mildon, *Inclusive Growth: Future-proof your business by creating a diverse workplace* (Rethink Press, 2020), p.26

38 V Myers, 'How to overcome our biases? Walk boldly toward them' (Ted Talk, 2016), www.ted.com/talks/

verna_myers_how_to_overcome_our_biases_walk_boldly_
toward_them?language=en, accessed 08/08/2022

39 W Kahn, 'Psychological conditions of personal engagement
    and disengagement at work', *Academy of Management
    Journal*, 33/4 (1990), 692–724, www.jstor.org/stable/256287,
    accessed 08/08/2022

40 See endnote 29

41 S Covey, *The 7 Habits of Highly Effective People* (Simon and
    Schuster, 2004), p.255

42 N Wolchover, 'The Original Human Language Like
    Yoda Sounded' (Live Science, 2011), www.livescience.
    com/16541-original-human-language-yoda-sounded.html,
    accessed 13/10/2022

43 Elisabeth Kübler-Ross Foundation, 'Kübler-Ross Change
    Curve®', www.ekrfoundation.org/5-stages-of-grief/
    change-curve, accessed 03/10/2022

44 N Molefi, J O'Mara and A Richter, *Global Diversity, Equity
    and Inclusion Benchmarks: Standards for organizations
    around the world*© (The Centre for Global Inclusion,
    2021. Used with permission. All rights reserved.), www.
    centreforglobalinclusion.org/file_download/inline/
    a1564bf0-9b5d-469a-a516-c6d438c79609, accessed
    01/09/2022

Further Reading

Gender

Ferguson, Sian, 'Privilege 101: A quick and dirty guide' (Everyday Feminism, 2014), www.everydayfeminism.com/2014/09/what-is-privilege, accessed 03/09/2022

Gender Decoder: https://gender-decoder.katmatfield.com, accessed 03/09/2022

Helgesen, Sally and Marshall Goldsmith, *How Women Rise* (Random House, 2019)

McGuire, Mary, *The Female Edge* (Rethink Press, 2021)

Schwartz, Ariel, 'Here Are All the Quantifiable Reasons You Should Hire More Women' (Fast Company, 2014), www.fastcompany.com/3028227/here-are-all-the-quantifiable-reasons-you-should-hire-more-women, accessed 03/09/2022

Sieghart, Mary Ann, *The Authority Gap* (Black Swan, 2022)

Race

DiAngelo, Robin, *White Fragility* (Penguin, 2019)

Oluo, Ljeoma, *So You Want to Talk About Race* (Seal Press, 2020)

LGBTQ+

Schadendorf, Jens, *GaYme Changer* (LID Publishing, 2021)

Neurodiversity

Kirby, Amanda and Theo Smith, *Neurodiversity at Work: Drive innovation, performance and productivity with a neurodiverse workforce* (Kogan Page, 2021)

Bias-busting

Burdick, Annie, *Unconscious Bias: Everything you need to know about our hidden prejudices* (Summersdale, 2021)

Diversity, equity and inclusion

Bolger, Meg, 'Privilege for Sale' (Social Justice Toolbox), www.socialjusticetoolbox.com/activity/privilege-for-sale, accessed 03/09/2022

Brown, Jennifer, *How to Be an Inclusive Leader* (Berrett-Koehler Publishers, 2019)

Catalyst, 'Quick Take: Why diversity and inclusion matter' (Catalyst, 2018), www.catalyst.org/knowledge/why-diversity-and-inclusion-matter, accessed 03/09/2022

Centre for Global Inclusion: www.centreforglobalinclusion.org, accessed 03/09/2022

Fanshawe, Simon, *The Power of Difference* (Kogan Page, 2022)

Jacob, Kathryn et al, *Belonging* (Bloomsbury, 2020)

Robbins, Mike, *Bring Your Whole Self to Work: How vulnerability unlocks creativity, connection and performance* (Hay House Inc, 2018)

Sweeney, Charlotte and Fleur Bothwick, *Inclusive Leadership: The definitive guide to developing and executing an impactful diversity and inclusion strategy* (Financial Times/Pearson Education, 2016)

Tapia, Andrés and Alina Polonskaia, *The 5 Disciplines of Inclusive Leaders: Unleashing the power of all of us* (Korn Ferry, 2020)

Appendix

Core Values Exercise

The foundations of life are built upon values that have been created from childhood by our families, communities and our interactions with others. Personal or core values are deeply held beliefs comprised of our convictions, standards and ethics. Some of these are formed early and stay with us for our entire life, while others are formed at a later stage. Knowing our core values is important because they assert a profound influence over the course of our lives. They give us meaning and direction and without them, we would be lost.

The reason we behave the way we do towards others will be based on our values. When you think about it, all of our relationships are coloured by our values. As you move towards building a more equitable and inclusive workplace for others, you need to understand the values driving you, and by extension what values might be affecting other people.

Thank you to Lucy McCarraher of Rethink Press for kind permission to reproduce the exercise here. The full list of values to choose from is available at www. agents2change.com/theinclusionedge.

Uncovering your core values

1. Look through the long list of values and pick out your top twenty. Don't take too much time deciding, as you will find that this is largely an intuitive exercise. You may find that you could choose more than twenty. Don't worry about the ones that don't make the list, the exercise has a way of evening out your choices.

2. As you circle your preferred values (remember there are no good or bad choices) notice if themes emerge.

3. When you have your top twenty, review them and then decide which are the six most important values. Again, gut is more helpful than head here. Which feel like the right values to you?

4. When you have the top six, be ready to share them with your colleagues and team members.

If that feels like a big jump, start with a partner or close friend. Share the values and explain why they are important to you. Ask for their opinion. Do your choices surprise them, or are they in line with how they see you?

5. Choose one value out of the top six that is your core value, the value by which all your actions and thoughts must be measured by. This value will be how you describe yourself, how you work and also how you set priorities in how you will lead out in diversity and inclusion.

My DE&I Manifesto

Use the template below as a guide, but change as you think best for your circumstances and role.

I [insert your name here] choose to be a leader that promotes diversity, equity and inclusion positively among my employees. I will address inequalities as I see them and provide a positive role model to help people with seen and unseen differences to thrive and grow at work.

I will educate myself, my team and my peers on the issues in inequality, discrimination and unconscious bias using the resources available within and beyond my organisation.

I will stand up for the rights of minorities.

I will strive to ensure that my behaviours always embody belonging.

I am open to feedback to help me better understand the diverse needs of my employees and how I can best support them.

I am an ally and will be a helpful resource to any employee that identifies with a diverse characteristic and I will do what I can to support them and their career aspirations.

I will be led by my core value of [insert your core value here].

I will adhere to the organisation's values, but I will particularly embody [insert value here] so that I can better serve my employees and create a culture of belonging.

I will use data and information to understand the areas of most need in terms of diversity and fair representation and make it a priority to address these.

I will listen to the diverse experiences of my employees and learn how to create a better, more equal workplace that celebrates the differences in everyone.

Job Profile: DE&I Ambassador

To be a DE&I ambassador, your most important quality is a passion and interest in diversity and how to bring about equality for everyone. You will be someone who is comfortable talking to people, keen to share experiences (your own and other people's) and motivated to put on employee engagement events such as lunch-and-learn, or cultural celebrations that promote belonging.

Key responsibilities include:

- Act as the lead person in coordinating activities with other DE&I ambassadors across the business

- Host DE&I forum meetings on occasion, in collaboration with other DE&I ambassadors

- Train all new employees on an introduction to DE&I and share the online learning resources with them

- Actively educate employees on matters of DE&I, including relevant news, reading materials, case studies and videos to promote inclusivity within the workplace

- Help formulate the DE&I strategy going forward

- Plan future sessions/topics/training with the other DE&I ambassadors and the affinity groups

- Attend training/workshops as required to stay up to date on DE&I issues

- Champion and model diversity and inclusion across the wider company

- Support the talent teams in refining recruitment strategy and how we can attract diverse talent

How To Find And Be An Ally

How be an ally

As a majority leader, you can become a great ally for diverse talent in your organisation and help them to find a way to career success. Here are some suggestions of how you might go about this:

- Become a buddy or mentor for an employee who would be considered in the minority – either a long-standing employee or a newly appointed leader. Help them to navigate the organisation, know its politics and identify the influencers they should engage.

- Take some unconscious bias training and become more aware of gender and other biases that you may inadvertently hold.

- Consider platforms or forums that diverse talent can contribute to, lead or create to showcase their skills.

- Be more observant in meetings of how well balanced the contributions are between different groups. Look for ways you can intervene and redress the balance.

- In promotion discussions, consider the balance of nominations. Does it truly reflect the employee population? Use your influence to address this.

- Look at your own hiring and progression decisions. Do you look at capability before any other quality and does this show up in the people that you support and promote?

- Go out of your way to ask female leaders and other diverse talent what support you can give them and follow through on the action.

How to find an ally

Allies are those people that share a common purpose with you and will back you up publicly and support your aims. Look for allies within your organisation, but also look across boundaries to peers in other organisations, previous bosses and new contacts through networking. Company events, professional bodies and affinity groups are all great places to find your allies.

When you meet your allies, be clear about what you want from them, but also what you have to give as well. Think about an ally or sponsor as someone who benefits from knowing your work, but who will also benefit you through their influence.

Your ally can help you to see:

- Where you could be in three to five years' time

- Where your skills are a good match

- What areas you need to develop

- Who you need to know

- What additional skills you need to hone

- Where you might gain additional exposure or experience to accelerate your career

The best allies are long-term buddies. They are there for you through thick and thin and across organisational boundaries. Your old boss, for example, might be a perfect ally. Remember to keep your ally updated on your progress and if they have helped you with something, remember that all-important thank you.

Adapted from *The Female Edge*, Mary McGuire (Rethink Press, 2021)

Checklist Of Behaviours That Promote Psychological Safety

1. Open meetings by ensuring that everyone has introduced themselves.

2. Start the agenda with a round robin of updates from everyone. Try to be the last person in the room to speak.

3. Clarify roles and deliverables across the team.

4. Spotlight successes and praise good work.

5. Encourage the team to speak up if they have any concerns or doubts.

6. Acknowledge your own fallibility. If you make mistakes, own up to them and thank people for pointing them out.

7. Encourage feedback by being open to it. Ask regularly how you are doing and ask your team what they need from you as their leader.

8. Take criticism gracefully. Always thank the person, reflect on it and then decide if it is of value.

9. Look for ways to recognise great work through habits like thank-you emails, spot bonuses and awarding paid time off when something great has been delivered.

Acknowledgements

Publishing a book is a marathon not a sprint and I'm indebted to many people who have supported me every step of the way.

This book was influenced by the work I am privileged to do with my many global clients. It is to them I want to say thank you for all the wonderful experiences I have had over the last thirty years. You have opened my eyes, broadened my horizons and helped me to always strive to do better every day.

An author relies on their readers to tell them what is good and not so good about their work. I had a wonderful set of beta-readers who diligently reviewed the early manuscript, gave me very constructive feedback on how to improve and provided early endorsement.

Thank you to Besmira Tuga, Colin Daley, Jo Hatfield, Justine Harris, Mark Blythe, Rob Mason and Steven Cochrane.

I am indebted to the team at Rethink Press for their outstanding support. Eve Makepeace managed the publishing process seamlessly; Tess Jolly was editor extraordinaire; and Jane Dixon-Smith yet again created a wonderful book cover design. I also want to thank the Rethink founders, Lucy McCarraher and Joe Gregory, for their guidance and mentoring.

Thank you to my partner Joy, for being you, allowing me to be me and for everything you do for us.

Finally, thank you to you my readers and past and future clients, who are always teaching me so much about living the best life you can, from your own authentic voice.

The Author

For the last twenty years, Mary McGuire has travelled the world working with global companies on their most challenging issues. Perhaps the biggest of these is how to create a culture of belonging in a volatile world.

Using insights from her early career in social work and a deep understanding of human behaviour, Mary has created a practical approach to DE&I for the busy business leader. The BELONG model is based on her leadership development programmes, providing a pathway for leaders to become more comfortable managing diverse teams.

In addition to being a published author, a Chartered Fellow of CIPD (UK) and holding an MSc and MBA, Mary is a speaker, coach and charity trustee. She leads with kindness and believes passionately in equality for everyone.

She lives in Oxfordshire with her loving partner, Joy, and when she is not writing, coaching and advising, Mary will be found in a corner reading a book.

in www.linkedin.com/in/marymcguire

🐦 https://twitter.com/MarytmcGuire

9 781781 337240